tea in the east

tea
in the
east

CAROLE MANCHESTER

Photographs by Walter Smalling, Jr.

HEARST BOOKS
NEW YORK

To my father, and in memory of my mother, tea lovers both

It is the policy of William Morrow and Company, Inc., and its imprints and affiliates,
recognizing the importance of preserving what has been written, to print the books we
publish on acid-free paper, and we exert our best efforts to that end.

Library of Congress Cataloging-in-Publication Data

Manchester, Carole.
    Tea in the East / Carole Manchester.
        p.   cm.
    Includes index.
    ISBN 0-688-13243-X (acid-free paper)
    1. Tea—Asia.   2. Tea—History. I. Title.
    GT2907.A78M35 1996
394. 1'5—dc20

95-47841
CIP

Printed in the United States of America

First Edition

1 2 3 4 5 6 7 8 9 10

BOOK DESIGN BY DONNA AGAJANIAN

acknowledgments

One expects impediments and impasses beyond control on a pilgrimage to alien environs, no matter how carefully planned the venture. There were many trying times rummaging through the obscure domains of tea, but at journey's end I look back on the adversities as fond adventures. What is sharpest in my mind though are the fortuitous crossings of paths with the most extraordinary individuals, staunch devotees of tea—planters, pluckers, brokers, blenders, producers, promoters, and tea lovers, some with a long history in the business, some passionate on the subject, all generous with their time and willing to share their knowledge, experience, and love of tea. They enriched my Asian travels and were key to the production of this book. There were those close to home as well. Thank you to all with special thanks to:

My agent, Gayle Benderoff, who suggested I write another tea book, and my editor, Harriet Bell, who gave superb guidance. My adoptive editor, Gail Kinn, who picked up the pieces and made them fit together so thoughtfully when Harriet moved on. The gifted designers who made such a lovely book, Donna Agajanian, and Morrow's design director, Linda Kocur.

Walter Smalling for wonderful photographs and being such a good friend and traveling companion.

Ip Wing Chi for sharing his tea knowledge and cups of tea, and for guiding me through China's tea country. George Chang for his assistance and photographs. Sally Harpole for many helpful suggestions regarding China and its tea traditions. Anita Wong of the Flagstaff House Museum of Tea Ware for archival photographs.

Kumiko Hilano and Setsuko Okura for helping me coordinate my work in Japan.

Nosh Anzar, Shama Habibullah, and Madhavan Nambiar, formerly director of the Tea Board of India, for invaluable introductions and guidance in India.

Krishna Kumar and Saeed Kidwai at Tata Tea Limited for their hospitality and assistance in Calcutta and Munnar.

Gillem Sandys-Lumsdaine and his associates in Calcutta at Williamson Magor & Co., S. K. Dutta at Carritt Moran & Co., Harish Parekh at J. Thomas & Co., Partha Mazumdar at Rossell Industries, Lubna Huq of The Tea Board of India, Raaj Waiba and Darjeeling tea friends at the West Bengal Tea Development Corporation and Rungneet Tea Estate. All showed me interesting aspects of the tea business.

Good friends Bharath Ramamrutham and Dr. A. U. Ramakrishnan for their assistance in Bombay.

Pankaj M. Baliga of the Taj Mahal Hotel for his kindness and patience with my many requests, and the splendid Taj chefs for superb teas.

The Consulate General of India, Government of India Tourist Office, Air India, and Cox & Kings for travel assistance.

Nirmala de Mel for introductions, travel assistance, and a charming tea at her guest house, Tissawewa in Sri Lanka.

For inspiring tea tables and sharing recipes and cups of tea in China, Hong Kong, and Kowloon: Marlin Allies, Alan Chan, the China Club, Charlotte Horstmann & Gerald Godfrey Ltd., Cai Ting Hui, Grand Hyatt Hong Kong, Thomas K. Lee, Luk Yu Teahouse, Michael Ng, Tony Ngan, Graem J. Reading, Tony Kin Woon, Yung Hua Yang, and Zitan.

In Japan: Toshiko Fukuda, Tae Hashimoto, Hyotei, Ippodo Tea Co. Ltd., Kikuya, Junko Koshino, Jurgen Lehl, Matsuzaki, John McGee, Minkaen, Momiji-An, Kazuko and Tadashi Morita, Takashimaya Co. Ltd., "Tea Leaves" at Matsuya, "Tokyo," Toraya, and Seimei Tsuji.

In India: S. Azhar Ahsan, Dr. Bilkiz Alladin, Sono Apparao, Prem Chenoy, Darjeeling Club (Planters), High Range Club, Begum Ghausia Hussain, Sanjay Kapur at Aap Ki Pasand, Sujaya Menon, Venu and Sarala Menon, Jayanti L. Naik, Gopalan and Radha Nair, Krishna Nambiar, Popli & Popli, Parul Shah, Farida Sheriff, Shilpa Shroff, Maharaj Swaroop Singh and Rani Usha Devi, Naheed Sorabjee, Tollygunge Club, and the Dhendup Wangchuk family.

In Sri Lanka: The Galle Face Hotel, Hellbodde Estate, Hill Club, and The Villa.

In New York: Ellen Greaves at Takashimaya, Russian Tea Room, T, and Toraya.

Finally, thanks to my husband, Shunna Pillay, for his patience and support throughout the project.

acknowledgments

contents

introduction

"THERE ARE A THOUSAND DIFFERENT appearances of tea leaves. Some have creases like the leathern boot of a Tartar horseman, curl like the dewlap of a mighty bullock, unfold like a mist rising out of a ravine, gleam like a lake touched by a zephyr, and be wet and soft like fine earth newly swept by rain."

LU YU, *CH'A CHING*, 780

*T*HEA IS THE BOTANICAL name for the tea plant, first used by Engelbert
Kaempfer (1651–1716), later to be classified as *Thea sinensis*, then as
Thea viridis for green tea and *Thea bohea* for black. There was much debate
also about whether the Assamese tea plant was the same as the Chinese. It
finally took the International Code of Botanical Nomenclature to resolve the
years of confusion. The body decreed that all Theas were actually camellias,
and one and the same, and that tea's real name is *Camellia sinensis*.

The evergreen tea tree has leathery, serrated, strongly veined leaves that
sprout from short-channelled stalks off a stem that has numerous leafy
branches. The underside of a young leaf is covered with fine hairs, which dis-
appear as the leaf ages. The tree, which can grow as tall as fifteen feet, is
pruned to bush size to encourage growth of the young leaves, or flush, from
which tea is made.

There are three classifications of tea—green, oolong, and black. The clas-
sification is determined by the method of processing the leaves. Green teas
are unfermented. Twenty pounds of leaves at a time are either lightly pan-
fired, stirred, and tossed in a wok-like metal pan for a half hour or more or
steamed after plucking to prevent oxidation (fermentation). Oolongs are
semi-fermented. The leaves are withered in the shade for about five hours,
then pan-fired for ten minutes, rolled, and twisted. (Twisted leaves give a
more flavorful brew than flat leaves.) Next the leaves are oxidized. Oxidation
determines the color, flavor, and body of the tea. Five pounds of leaves at a
time are refired in hourglass-shaped bamboo baskets for three hours, which
ends the oxidation. They are refired up to twelve hours before packing. Black
teas are fermented. The leaves are withered up to twenty-four hours, then
rolled, sifted, spread out on a spotless surface for a couple of hours to oxidize,
fired—a process that dries the leaves in hot air machines—and finally sorted
by size, which determines the grade of the tea. The unique white tea is in a
class by itself, produced only in China of mature buds from a rare tea bush
found in Fukien. It is neither oxidized nor rolled.

The original tea jungles of wild camellias were indigenous to the monsoon
enclave of southeastern Asia, northern Siam (Thailand), eastern Burma
(Myanmar), southwest China, northeast India, and upper Indochina. The
aboriginal tribes inhabiting this region gathered and used the leaves of the
miang, the wild tea trees growing on their native hills, since the beginning of
time. Tea was a vegetable source essential to their diet, and they steamed and
fermented small bundles of leaves for chewing. The tribesmen of the hill districts bordering southwestern China brewed a beverage by boiling raw green
leaves of the miang in kettles over outdoor fires. The rest of China adopted

the idea and turned this early, simple beverage, drunk more for its supposed health benefits than for taste, into the ennobling drink it is today.

China was for centuries the sole producer of tea and uncommunicative about the methods of cultivation of her precious drink, but through trade and cultural exchange her secrets were revealed and spread to other countries. By the nineteenth century, tea growing had spread to Japan, Java, India, Ceylon (Sri Lanka), Russia, Persia (Iran), Turkey, Indochina, Formosa (Taiwan), Sumatra, and the Fiji Islands. Some of these countries have become significant growers, but China still cultivates more varieties and remains one of the major suppliers of the choice Asian teas, along with India, Sri Lanka, and Japan. I chose to travel to these four countries, which have long produced the much-loved teas of the world—green, oolong, black, and white teas from China, greens from Japan, and black teas from India and Sri Lanka. These forerunners of the tea business not only continue to provide us with tea but also established the tea customs adopted by the world's tea drinkers. They are steeped in tea tradition and share a similar affinity for the brew, but their tea styles have unique distinctions.

In China, I was struck by the simplicity of taking tea on a small farm. A family picks two baskets of tea leaves and tosses them onto their linoleum-covered table, where two young women sort out the undesirable bits. A wood fire is stoked in the kitchen stove. The dark green leaves are dumped into a metal wok, which is set into the burner. The pan-firing is accomplished quickly, deft hands tossing the leaves, rubbing them against the sides of the wok. Then, in about half an hour, the tea leaves, now dry and twisted, are infused in glasses of hot water. The taste of China is in the glass.

In Japan, less is more, and the sparse presentation the quintessence of elegance in understatement. At a business meeting, a refined woman serves green tea with steamed fava beans on a red lacquer plate. The combination seems odd at first, but the vegetative tastes of tea and bean marry well. The first sights in India are the numerous tea shops and the tea vendors hurrying through the streets with steaming kettles. The operation of the hole-in-the-wall shops is casual, where all day long the tea wallahs, who seem like schoolboys, keep vats of sweet, milky tea going. Rich buffalo milk curd sweetened with brown sugar syrup is a favorite with tea in Sri Lanka.

Although each country has different customs and styles, the ritual of making tea remains the same. The water is heated to the correct temperature, the teapot is warmed, the precise amount of tea leaves are infused for the prescribed length of time, and we are in a tea mind ready to drink the world's most satisfying brew from glass, cup, or bowl.

china

DURING THE SUNG DYNASTY, POET LI

Chi Lai cited three great evils that beset the land:

"the spoiling of gallant youths through bad edu-

cation; the degradation of good art through

incompetent criticism; and the waste of fine tea

through careless making."

THE ORIGIN OF TEA in China is obscured in its revered antiquity. The oldest legend of the first brew, dated 2737 B.C., is ascribed to Emperor Shen Nung, the Divine Healer, a practical man who discovered that boiling water before drinking it prevented illness. As the story goes, one day a fortuitous breeze snapped the leaves from the branches of a wild camellia tree and dropped them into a pot of boiling water being prepared for the emperor, and thus the first brew. There are many such undocumented claims to tea's beginnings, and to disregard them would be ignoring the Eastern tradition of oral rather than written history. Tea is alluded to in 50 B.C. in "Servant Rules," a contract between employer Wang Piu and his servant, in which one of the servant's listed duties is to buy and prepare tea.

The earliest credible documented record of tea is a definition chronicled in the *Erh Ya*, an ancient Chinese dictionary, noted by scholar Kuo P'o in A.D. 350. Tea is listed as *kia*, or *k'u t'u* (called *ch'a* sometime after 725), and defined as a beverage made by boiling leaves. The brew in Kuo P'o's day was a bitter medicinal drink made from raw green tea leaves plucked, pressed into cakes, roasted until reddish in color, then pounded into tiny pieces and boiled in a kettle of water flavored with onion, ginger, and orange. This concoction was used as a remedy for distemper, stomach disorders, lethargy, bad eyesight, and countless other ailments until the sixth century, when emperors, priests, scholars, and members of the upper class began to drink it as a refreshment.

As tea producers learned new methods of improving the leaf after the publication of Lu Yu's tea classic, the *Ch'a Ching*, in A.D. 780, during the Tang dynasty in China, a better quality of tea emerged and, consequently, wider tea appreciation. Roasted cake tea, shredded and boiled in water with a pinch of salt, became a national drink. The increasing demand for the beverage encouraged farmers in many provinces to allot small patches of land to tea growing. Tea gardens, formerly exclusive to the Sichuan hills, extended down into the Yangtze valley and along the seaboard.

The *Ch'a Ching* disclosed everything there was to know about tea. In three volumes and ten chapters, the distinguished scholar Lu Yu, a foundling brought up by Buddhist monks, revealed the botanical origin of tea, with historical references, a list of producing districts, techniques for proper cultivation, instructions on manipulation of the leaves, and descriptions of implements for its proper preparation, infusion, and drinking. Lu Yu ended with a general summary and a memo to tea merchants advising them on how to use his masterpiece, for it was they who sponsored the treatise to spread knowledge on the cultivation of tea and, ultimately, promote their product.

Through tireless research and piecing together scattered bits of information, Lu Yu presented his study simply and clearly. In the process, he discovered a spirituality in the preparation, drinking, and appreciation of tea. Canonized in his own time by his peers as the patron saint of tea, Lu Yu saw in the tea ritual the same harmony and order that rule all other aspects of life and set a standard of practice, a tea code, which brought tea to an ideal, out of which came the Japanese tea ceremony.

Lu Yu listed twenty-four implements as essential to the preparation of tea, from stove, firing basket, poker, tongs, boiler, boiler stand, and green bamboo for baking tea to paper bag to keep it fresh to grinder, sieve, measure, water tank, and more, including china, favoring the celadon-glazed Yueh ware. In his general summary, Lu Yu allowed concessions, but only under certain circumstances. "If tea is prepared under pine trees and on a rock, then the sideboard is not needed; . . . if a stream is nearby, then the water tank, slop basin, and water-straining bag are not needed. . . ." But, he concludes, "If, however, one of the twenty-four implements is missing in an aristocratic family inside the city, then tea cannot be prepared." These requirements for preparing the brew threw artisans into a frenzy of creating magnificent examples of ornamental pulverizers, ewers, tea bowls, and cups, as well as special cabinets in which to store them. At this time during the Tang dynasty, the hard, nonporous, translucent porcelain we call china was invented, and the genius of China's artisans elevated the process to unequaled beauty of form and color, which influenced all ceramic arts for tea.

China maintained the standards set by Lu Yu for the remainder of the Tang dynasty (618–907) and through the Sung dynasty (960–1279), a period when China's tea culture was at its height. Invasions, changing dynasties, and political upheavals would compromise the ideal, but the habit of proper tea drinking was established.

Cake tea evolved to leaf tea by 850, but during the Sung dynasty, dried tea leaves were ground into a powder and whipped in hot water with a bamboo whisk in ceramic tea bowls glazed in dark colors and embellished with carved, appliqué, and resist motif design. For the first time, tea was taken without salt or other additives. Tea cultivation increased with new gardens in the provinces of Anhui, Fujian, and Guangxi. Elaborate teahouses opened in all the cities of China, and everyone drank tea. Among the intellectuals and aristocrats, tea was not just a beverage, but a stylish social ritual as well. The caliber of personal tea collections became a testimonial to social status. Proper etiquette required serving tea to visitors in rooms set aside for the purpose. There were tea parties and tea tournaments to judge the merits of eagerly sought new varieties. The tea-loving Emperor Kiasung (1101–1126) spent freely to obtain new and rare teas, and out of twenty declared the white tea the most delicate in flavor. Tea enthusiasts held contests, the winner being the one whose bowl of whipped tea had the most lasting froth. Young tea lovers met to drink and discuss tea, to listen to music, paint pictures, and write and recite poems between sessions of tea drinking. They gathered in teahouses set in idyllic surroundings, in gardens and in the mountains. Buddhist priests assembled in their temples before a portrait of their founder, Bodhidharma, and solemly drank powdered tea from a communal bowl. Tea drinking was a gracious, refined addition to Chinese life that lasted for two hundred years.

The beautiful life might have continued were it not for the nomadic Mongol tribes from the northwest, who, after constant incursions across the vast expanse of harsh grasslands, the formidable Gobi Desert, and the Great Wall, finally succeeded in conquering Peking (Beijing) in 1215. For centuries, the Chinese had been supplying these enemies with a crude brick tea. The Mongols craved the tea made from compressed leaves, twigs, and sweepings of just about anything gathered in the process, as the soupy slop substituted for the lack of green vegetables in their meat and milk diet. The Chinese traded tea for horses as a ploy to keep the barbarians grounded, and tea-horse offices were established to oversee the business. All this ended when Genghis Khan united the Mongol hordes and swept into northern China with an invincible force.

The south was spared until Genghis's grandson, Kublai Khan, overthrew the Southern Sung dynasty in 1279 to complete the conquest of China. Cultural life and the refinement of tea drinking ended as the Sung knew it. The Mongols did not care for the subtleties of tea. They added cream to their bowl and ate a variety of nuts with it as part of a meal, a precursor to dim sum (typical Cantonese savory snacks of, for example, glutinous rice dumplings filled with fish, chicken, or pork or finely chopped fish, meat, or vegetables wrapped in thin dough).

Kublai Khan became the first emperor of the Yuan dynasty (1279–1368) and made Peking the capital. The China he ruled was the largest country in the world, and by the thirteenth century its cities were more prosperous than any in Europe. Marco Polo amazed the Europeans when he chronicled the splendors of China in writings of his travels, but he never mentioned tea. An explanation might be that Marco Polo's hosts were the Tartar rulers, and they were not interested in the customs of their subjugated citizens. Manufacturers, undeterred by the Mongols' lack of interest in tea, invented a method of flavoring the leaves and introduced teas scented with fragrant orchid, lotus, rose, orange, and cassia blossoms. Tea was still the national drink but it was no longer held in the high esteem it had been under the Sung, and never would be again.

The death of Kublai Khan ended the Tartar reign. China was then ruled by the Ming, an isolationist-minded dynasty (1368–1643) that saw China as culturally, economically, and spiritually superior to the outside world and attempted to bring back tea and its ceremonies as part of the cultural renaissance. During this era, the Chinese invented the process of manufacturing green tea and introduced the steeping method of brewing tea we practice today. The leaves were steeped in bowls, or covered cups of thin, translucent porcelain in shades of white, until around 1500, when the Yixing teapot came into favor. The small teapot, made of unglazed red or brown stoneware, was well suited to bring out the flavor, color, and aroma of the leaves, and its size made it easy to balance the ratio of water to tea. Tea was sipped from tiny handleless cups that complemented the size of the teapot.

When China was conquered once again, this time by the Manchus, who set up the Qing dynasty (1644–1912), the Yixing pot was still in fashion. Pewter pots were favored too, because they kept tea warmer longer, and porcelain because it gave a feeling of cleanliness. It was during the Qing rule that tea manufacturers invented special methods to control tea fermentation, which resulted in black and oolong teas. From then on there were more varieties of tea, and as news of the beverage spread, more countries became curious about the China drink.

The Europeans' obsession with discovering the sea route to Asia was finally realized when the Portuguese landed in China in 1516. The conservative Chinese rulers, wary of strangers as always, would have little to do with them, but in time the newcomers convinced the emperor that they had not come as invaders, but rather as traders. They were finally allowed to set up a base in Macau in 1557, mainly as a reward for ridding the China Sea of pirates. The Dutch, British, and Spanish followed in the waning years of the Ming and the beginning of the Qing dynasty. The Qing, like the Ming, conservative in their thinking, were cool to the advances of the latest interlopers, and it was not until 1685 that they finally agreed to do business with them. The Qing despised the Europeans on the one hand, but, on the other, were not so repelled as to give up the prospect of profiting from trading with them. These outer barbarians were kept at arm's length. Business was conducted only in the distant port of Canton, far from Peking, the political center in the north.

In 1702, the emperor appointed a *hoppo*, or emperor's merchant, as the sole negotiator with whom the Europeans had to trade. An account by Dr.

Toogood Downing, a British tea merchant, tells of the hoppo's visit to an English factory. The regal nobleman, a high-ranking dignitary flanked by secretaries, advisers, and linguists, arrived dressed in robes of the finest embroidered silks and sat on a small throne at a table where a full English breakfast was set before him. "The old man eyed the good things upon the table, and, as he had the whole of them to himself, no one presuming to take a seat, he whispered to his attendant to fetch them for him. As each dish was brought successively, and held up to his eye, he examined it very carefully all around as an object of great curiosity, and then languishingly shook his head, as a sign for it to be taken away. Thus he proceeded for a considerable time, until he had looked at everything on the table, without finding a single article suitable to his delicate stomach." The story ends, ". . . when the table had been entirely ransacked, he shook his head once more in sign of disapproval, and then called for a cup of tea. . . ."

As business with the foreigners accelerated, the hoppo devised a more efficient arrangement in 1704, admitting up to thirteen Chinese merchants to share in the tea trade. These men were called the Hong merchants because they owned *hongs* (warehouses for foreign trade) and paid the hoppo what amounted to customs duties in return for the privilege. They also had to bear the responsibility for all that went wrong, and were fined when anything did. The Hong merchants fretted that they would lose everything in the ups and downs of brokering between the Chinese and the British, but, as it turned out, they amassed immense fortunes as middlemen and lived the lives of kings in grandiose mansions.

In time, the British became unhappy in their business dealings with the Chinese. The monies the British spent on tea, porcelain, and silk far exceeded what little they took in from the wool and spices they sold in return, and they were obliged to make up the difference in silver coinage. Consequently, the British embarked on a scheme in 1773 to addict the Chinese to Indian opium, for by now they controlled India. Success came swiftly. Increasing opium addiction drained the Chinese coffers, tilting the balance of payment in Britain's favor. In 1800, to stem the tide, the Chinese emperor banned trade with the foreigners, but the British ignored the prohibition. To assert their authority, the Chinese seized twenty thousand chests of opium in Canton in 1839, infuriating the British, who in turn attacked the Chinese in the first of four Opium Wars, instigated at the smallest trumped-up pretext. The Chinese were made to pay large sums of money as war indemnities and they in turn made the Hong merchants pay part of the cost. The fourth and last war was fought in 1859–1860. An "Unequal Treaty" was signed after each war, always in favor of the foreigners. Customs tariffs on imported goods were sharply reduced and more Chinese ports were opened to the foreigners, who gave themselves the right to travel freely anywhere in China.

Tea had reached the Asian countries on the overland route as early as the time of the Sung dynasty, but now, with the opening of China, there was a rush to introduce the China drink to the West. Tea had to be shipped as quickly as possible, for the freshest tea brought the most profit. The frigate ships, the "tea wagons" of the East India Company, were slow and no match for the American clipper ships that burst upon the scene in the 1830s. The multimasted vessels designed and built for speed suited the China tea trade perfectly. They had ample room for cargo and could make the trip on an average of ninety-two days from the New England coast to Canton, and eighty-one days back, bettering the frigates by two months. The British, with a monopoly on the tea trade, ignored the threat at first, but with the Americans cutting into their hold and amassing great fortunes after the first China opium war, they hurriedly built and launched their own clipper schooners, among them the *Ariel*, *Cutty Sark*, and *Thermopylae*, and so began the legendary tea races. There was no more important business pursuit in England than tea in the tea season, and the dashing tea-clippers were the focus of its attention. Telegrams relating the progress of the clippers were read with feverish anticipation in the tea brokerage house in Mincing Lane in London. Scores of sampling clerks converged on the docks as soon as news came that the clippers had passed Gravesend, on the south shore of the Thames River. A handsome profit awaited the consignee of the first arrival, and a winning crew received a five-hundred-pound bonus for the first tea of the season. By nine in the morning, samples were already being tasted in Mincing Lane, and once the dealers made their bids, the new season of congous (China black teas) would be on the shelves for sale in Liverpool and Manchester by next morning. The opening of the Suez Canal in 1869 shortened the commercial tea routes from the East, and, along with the advent of the steamship, ended the golden age of the clippers. The last China tea run was in 1871. By this time, tea was being grown in India, Ceylon, Japan, and elsewhere, and China's monopoly of the tea trade ended. A new tea era had begun.

Tea in China

"At the Jiangjianyue Teahouse, all kinds of special tea would be served and the entire building would be illuminated by big lamps shining bright yellow and every passerby would stop and admire the joyous atmosphere."

NAI DEWENG, *TRAVELLING ANCIENT HANGZHOU*, SUNG DYNASTY

the teahouse

Teahouses are to China what pubs are to England, familiar haunts where locals gather at any time of the day or night to meet friends, catch up on the news, discuss business, make deals, settle disputes, listen to stories, poetry, ballads, and opera; show off a pet bird in a cage, have one's ears cleaned, take a nap in a bamboo chair, and drink tea.

Teahouses appeared as early as the Tang dynasty and flourished in the cities of China during the Sung dynasty. Bouquets of seasonal flowers, fir, and pine scented the tearooms, calligraphy and paintings by famous artists decorated the walls, and tea was served in porcelain teaware carried on lacquered trays. Some teahouses offered singing lessons to the customers in exchange for playing musical instruments.

By the beginning of the Ming dynasty, teahouses, once the exclusive haunts of the wealthier class and literati, were open to everyone. Along with tea-trading firms, the teahouses of Hangzhou lined both sides of the streets, and Chengdu, the capital of Sichuan, boasted just as many. The Hangzhou teahouses were known for their scholarly atmosphere, while those in Chengdu emphasized storytelling, ballad singing, and *kuaiban* (rhythmic verses accompanied by bamboo clappers), a tradition that continues today.

Food was never served at teahouses, but fragrances were added to complement the brew, rose petals to black tea or jasmine to green tea. Symbolic teas were served on auspicious occasions. During the Lunar New Year, Yuanbao (gold ingot) tea was pressed on the teahouse customers for the first three days of the first lunar month. Fresh olives and kumquats were added to the tea and after one sip, it was said one's pocket would be filled with gold ingots all year round.

Teahouses remained popular through many dynasties and political

changes in China. They lost some of the luster of their early refined beginnings during the Manchus' rule in the Qing dynasty, and some of them degenerated into opium dens and brothels. But in one state or another, teahouses survived until the end of the 1940s, when Communist rule discouraged this favorite pastime. Since the late 1970s, however, a more relaxed attitude and a yearning for some of the old traditions have allowed teahouses in China to thrive again. Many teahouses have a regular clientele, such as "elderly" teahouses for retired seniors. Often the name describes the location. The Lakeview Teahouse, which faces West Lake in Hangzhou, is always filled with customers, on upstairs balconies and ground-level porches. Some play card games, others read newspapers, all drink tea. Inside, steaming kettles hiss and waiters move quickly to keep the teapots and cups filled.

The Dragon Well Teahouse, about six miles outside Hangzhou in a hilly region of Zhejiang Province, is located next to the famous spring of the same name. China's prized green teas, Lark's Tongue, Pi Lo Chun (Green Snail of Spring), and Long Jing (Dragon Well), are grown in this area. Only the most sophisticated tea drinkers can appreciate the distinctions. For the ultimate tea experience, these teas should be steeped in water drawn from the Dragon Well. Using the right water to make tea is as important as the tea itself, and water from springs in mountainous regions is the best. Of course, the quality of the water varies from one spring to the next. When brewed in water drawn from a spring called Hu Pao (Tiger Running), Pi Lo Chun and Long Jing taste sweeter than when brewed in water from the nearby Dragon Well. Pi Lo Chun is a rare tea produced just once a year in the early spring flush, and it is the most delicate of the three. Long Jing, once grown only for emperors, is best when picked fifteen days before the rain, early in the morning while the dew is on the buds. When steeped, it is a pale gold color and has a fresh, slightly grassy fragrance and flavor. The Dragon Well teas are also used in Hangzhou culinary specialties, such as freshwater shrimp stir-fried with tea leaves and carp stuffed with tea leaves.

The Ping Feng Teahouse in Longjing is a popular destination on Sunday afternoons, when Hangzhou residents drive out to drink the locally grown Dragon Well teas in a rural setting. There are at least forty-three varieties, divided into thirteen grades, the best of which are produced in early spring. At Ping Feng, the tea steeps directly in glasses, which are refilled whenever they reach the half-empty mark, eking out the last bit of flavor from the leaves. With refills included, the tea here is a good buy. Ping Feng is quieter on weekdays, when the only patrons are the local residents spending some of the day in the teahouse as they have always done.

The Humble Administrator's Teahouse, set in a Ming garden, is the oldest in Souzhou, one of many in this ancient canal city of scholars and artists, the oldest town in the Yangtze basin. The elegant teahouse, formerly a government official's private meeting room, is now open to the public, along with the surrounding gardens. Drinking tea here is particularly calming. The open floor-to-ceiling doors let in light, breezes, and the songs of birds from the garden.

In contrast, on a dusty back street of a village in Fujian, a province famous for its prized silvery, white-leafed tea, Silvery Tip Pekoe, as well as for Jasmine, Lapsang Souchong, and oolong teas—the latter the preferred in Fujian—tea tables spill out under an arcade from a teahouse tucked in a two-story tenement. Inside, kettles steam on the coal grate of a clay oven. The shelves, nooks, and crannies in and along the dingy walls are stacked with earthenware tea equipment. A ceramic tray holds a miniature teapot filled with tea leaves, surrounded by four doll-sized, handleless cups. The first brew is to wash the leaves, the second is to drink. In the early nineteenth century, tea was taken from the port of Amoy in Fujian and planted in Formosa (Taiwan), resulting in the China teas produced there, such as the semi-fermented Fancy Formosa Oolong, Pouchong (scented oolong), Pouchong-based Jasmine, fully fermented Tarry Souchong, Formosa Lapsang, Keemun, and unfermented pan-fired green teas. However, it is the distinctive, peachy oolong for which Formosa is famous.

The mountain people in southern Fujian and Taiwan make a compressed orange tea. Oranges are dried, the insides removed, and the peels filled with oolong tea leaves, then each is tied with a string marking off sections as on an orange and hung to dry in the sun. The aged tea keeps up to five years.

Further south in Yunnan, high in the mountains bordering Indochina, a teahouse furnished simply with foot-high bamboo stools and wooden tables serves the local black or compressed green teas to the regulars who come to chat, smoke, and play music. Yunnan's high-grown black teas are among the finest of China's blacks. Prized, too, is its aged compressed green tea, Pu Erh. Green teas are traditionally unfermented, but aged Pu Erh is an exception as it is a green tea fully fermented by introducing bacteria into the leaves and then aged after being pressed into bowl-shaped bricks or flat cakes. The best Pu Erh teas are aged twenty, forty, even up to sixty years. Pu Erh is considered a medicinal tea in Yunnan.

GREEN TEA–MARINATED CHICKEN SANDWICH

Makes 2 sandwiches

MARINADE

$^1/_2$ **cup soy sauce**

$^1/_2$ **cup maple syrup**

2 tablespoons green tea leaves

3 garlic cloves, minced

2 boneless skinless chicken breasts (about 6 ounces each)

1 small Japanese eggplant, sliced into $^1/_2$-inch-thick rounds

1 small red onion, thinly sliced

DRESSING

3 tablespoons plain yogurt

2 teaspoons Madras-style curry powder

1$^1/_2$ teaspoons ground coriander

1$^1/_2$ teaspoons ground cumin

1$^1/_2$ teaspoons ground cinnamon

$^1/_2$ teaspoon ground turmeric

$^1/_2$ teaspoon cayenne pepper, or to taste

4 slices sourdough bread, toasted

Prepare the marinade: In a medium bowl, combine the soy sauce, maple syrup, tea, and garlic. Add the chicken breasts. Cover and refrigerate for at least 12 hours, or overnight.

Position a rack in the upper third of the oven and preheat the oven to 350°F. Remove the chicken from the marinade and scrape off the tea and garlic. Strain the marinade into a medium saucepan and bring to a boil over medium heat. Cook for 10 minutes. Set aside.

Place the chicken breasts, eggplant, and onions on a large baking sheet. Bake, removing each ingredient as it is done and transferring to a platter, cover with aluminum foil to keep warm: Bake the onions until tender, about 10 minutes. Bake the eggplant, turning once, until golden brown, about 15 minutes, then brush with the marinade and bake until glazed, about 6 minutes. Bake the chicken breasts until firm when pressed in the thickest part, about 25 minutes.

Prepare the dressing: In a small bowl, combine all of the ingredients.

To assemble the sandwiches, spread the dressing on the slices of bread. Top 2 slices with the chicken, eggplant, and onion. Cover with the remaining bread. Cut each sandwich in half and serve immediately.

daily tea

"It was esteemed a wretched niggardliness to give only good words to those that come to their house, although they be strangers: At least they must have ch'a; and if the visit be anything long, here must be added some fruit or sweetmeats."

FATHER ALVARO SEMEDO, *THE HISTORY OF THE GREAT AND RENOWNED MONARCHY OF CHINA*, 1655

A VILLAGER'S TEA

There is an old Chinese saying that there are seven matters related to the starting of a family's life: firewood, rice, oil, salt, soy sauce, vinegar, and tea. Where the land and climate are compatible with tea plants, farmers allot space on their properties for growing tea along with their other crops. When the leaves are ready, they can be plucked, processed, and brewed within hours. In China, tea is as much the beverage of the common man as it is of a man of rank. Tea is the workingman's companion, an unpretentious, simple beverage, and taken for itself is the Chinese way. For some, a cup of tea, a bamboo chair, and a pet songbird are essential to daily life.

A PROFESSOR'S TEA

Tea lovers in China, through a connection, will always have the best tea available at any given time. Yung Hua Yang, a retired professor of Russian literature and language, is partial to Lion Rock, a green tea grown in the vicinity of the Dragon Well. Although his tea needs no accompaniments, watermelon seeds and sweets are served when there are guests. His wife, an artist, prepares the watermelon seeds by drying them in the sun and then boiling them in salted water with sugar, fennel, and aniseed.

A MUSICIAN'S TEA

During the Sung dynasty, scholars and artists were experts on the subtleties of tea drinking. They were the tea enthusiasts of the time and took great care in its preparation, calming their minds in the process. Tea drunk simply harmonized with their discussions on music, art, and poetry. Musician Tong Kin Woon prepares and drinks tea in this spirit. His Yixing teapot is from the seventeenth century, signed by artist Hai Meng-Chen. It rests on a sixteenth-century Zitan wood tray. The inkstone is from the twelfth century and the bamboo brush holder from the nineteenth century.

TEA IN A DAYBED

In the Ming dynasty, daybeds became works of art with elaborate fretwork and cane seating. They were elegant lairs in which to while away the hours, play card games, listen to music, read, and drink tea. Finely crafted of treasured woods, they were accessorized with decorative cushions. A nineteenth-century *taipan* (wealthy businessman) relaxed in this carved wood bed, cozied up with petit point cushions, Kang table, and cobalt-blue-and-white export porcelain teapot, as he sipped Keemun tea from his prized eighteenth-century porcelain teacups.

IN THE EXPORT STYLE

Red, black, and gold were the colors of China. One of China's royal teas is Ching Wo, a South China congou. South China congous are referred to as China's clarets. The coppery-colored Ching Wo from Fujian Province is a delicate tea with excellent body and aroma.

A TRAIN TEA

A cup of tea can be purchased even on a train trip, although a tea enthusiast with high standards will travel with a small teapot, *zhong* (covered teacup), four little teacups packed in a sock, and a favorite tea in a flat tin. With hot water supplied by the railway, tea is prepared as it would be at a tea ceremony.

TEA IN THE PROPER ENVIRONMENT

Surroundings are just as important to tea drinking as the right tea and proper equipment. The ideal environments are shaded terraces, quiet rooms, houses with bright windows, river bends, monasteries, pine woods, and bamboo groves, as prescribed in *The Story of the Flower House* by Lu Shusheng, written in the Ming dynasty.

In the cloistered world of the Suzhou Traditional Chinese Painting House, some of China's most esteemed artists work in quiet, light-filled rooms in a rambling single-storied structure built around a garden courtyard. Cai Ting Hue is a senior painter and engraver of steel, stone, and clay. Many of the Yixing teapots that line the shelves of his cluttered studio showcase his engraving skills. Surrounded by brushes, chisels, books, and other essentials to his craft, Cai drinks his tea directly from the spout of his teapot. Large red thermos bottles filled with hot water are as common as tea in China, always at the ready to steep a pot or glass of the brew.

Through lattice windows in a quiet room called The Place to Hear Pine Winds can be seen a Ming garden designed to mimic parts of rural South China. Great care has been taken to re-create southern nature in this garden to the north. A pine grove has been planted outside the windows, inspired by a historical biography of a southern dynastic family by Tao Hongjing, who wrote, "I have special affection for pine winds. There are pines growing in my garden court. I'm delighted to hear the sound of wind blowing through the pines." This is an environment for tea drinking.

Streams, ponds, and bridges are important elements in classical Chinese garden design. As the gardens were often created in small spaces, rocks were placed to simulate a mountain environment. Artists and scholars, the early tea drinkers who upheld the standards set for proper tea appreciation in China, placed great importance on the harmony of nature and tea. A painter, Nijan, in the Sung dynasty put tea leaves in a lotus flower, left them overnight in the closed blossom, and removed the scented leaves the next day to brew his lotus-flavored tea.

At a river bend, on a slow boat in China, dim sum, fresh shrimp, and tea are carried on board in a lacquered tiered basket. Tiny pellets of Gunpowder, a green tea from Anhui Province that the Chinese call Pearl Tea, are steeped in a porcelain teapot and sipped from tiny cups. The pellets open up as soon as the hot water is poured over them to reveal whole tea leaves. The brew, amber-colored in the cup and slightly acidic, goes well with the salty fare and is especially suited to drinking outdoors.

China Tea in Hong Kong

Tea style in Hong Kong mirrors that of mainland China. Those who left the mainland brought their tea habits along with them. The Cantonese introduced tea with dim sum. Oolong tea is favored among those from Fujian, where it is grown. The people with roots in Yunnan love their aged Pu Erh, and those from Beijing prefer Jasmine.

the teahouses

The Chinese teahouse tradition is carried on in Hong Kong at the Luk Yu teahouse on Stanley Street. The upmarket teahouse, which serves tea with dim sum, is a historic establishment on four floors in turn-of-the-century style, with ceiling fans, wood paneling, inlaid marble chairs, and burnished brass spitoons at each table. Tea is brewed at the tables in zhongs, which are kept filled by waiters who appear with kettles of hot water on spotting an uncovered cup—which communicates a desire for more water on the leaves. By noon the place is buzzing and jampacked with regulars and businessmen who have come for *yum cha* (tea and dim sum), lingering until well into the afternoon. Dim sum originated in Canton and has long been popular in Hong Kong, where the earthy Bolei (Cantonese for Pu Erh) tea is the preferred companion.

At the posh Grand Hyatt facing Victoria Harbour Bay on Harbour Road, going for yum cha is a quieter, more elegant experience. Dim sum is served on unmatched porcelain plates in a room furnished in the taipan style of the 1930s, a time best remembered for its high society and fine living.

STEAMED DUMPLINGS WITH SHRIMP AND BAMBOO SHOOTS

Makes 35 dumplings

1 pound medium shrimp, peeled and deveined

Vegetable oil for deep-frying

1 can (5 ounces) bamboo shoots, drained, rinsed, and chopped

$1/2$ teaspoon sugar

$1/2$ teaspoon salt

$1/8$ teaspoon ground white pepper

35 round wonton (gyoza) wrappers

Cornstarch for the baking sheet

Soy sauce for dipping

Cut one third of the shrimp into $1/4$-inch pieces and set aside. In a food processor fitted with the metal blade, process the remaining shrimp into a paste.

Pour enough vegetable oil into a saucepan to come $1^{1}/2$ inches up the sides. Heat the oil until it reaches 375°F. Add the chopped shrimp and cook until golden, about 1 minute. Transfer to paper towels to drain.

In a medium bowl, combine the cooked shrimp, ground shrimp, bamboo shoots, sugar, salt, and pepper.

Moisten the edges of a wonton wrapper with water. Place about 2 teaspoons of the shrimp mixture in the center of the wrapper. Fold in half so the edges meet, pressing to seal and pleating the edges of the wrapper. Place the dumpling on a cornstarch-dusted baking sheet. Repeat the procedure with the remaining wontons and filling, placing the dumplings so they do not touch.

In a large pot, bring about 2 inches of water to a full boil. Arrange the dumplings without touching in a stack of lightly oiled bamboo steaming baskets. Place the stack of baskets over the pot of boiling water, cover, and steam over medium heat until the dumplings are cooked through, about 12 minutes. (The dumplings can also be steamed in batches in a lightly oiled metal steaming rack placed over boiling water in a covered pot.) Serve warm with a small dish of soy sauce for dipping.

For members of the China Club, located on the top floors of the old Bank of China building, tea and dim sum is a strictly private affair. Its members, 70 percent Chinese, many from mainland China, take tea in a colonial Shanghai atmosphere. In the Grand Salon, midmorning dim sum is eaten with silver chopsticks and China tea is served in glasses. Ample armchairs covered with quaint antimacassars line one wall of the Long March Bar, where afternoon tea is served. Up on the Peak above the clusters of skyscrapers is the venerable Peak Café, often hidden in swirls of thick mist. This relic of old Hong Kong was once a sedan stop for patrons en route to their summer residences, and today it still caters to travelers. A moody but inviting place, it is a popular destination for tea and lunch. The fried noodles with a pot of Bolei are still a favorite.

A number of establishments in Hong Kong not only merchandise fine China teas but also demonstrate the art of tea preparation. Tai Koon-Lock Cha Tea Shop, just down the steps from the Cat Bazaar flea market on Ladder Street, is a particularly handsome establishment. A tea counter just inside the door displays select Yixing clay teapots, superior China teas, and teacups, with other tea paraphernalia along the opposite wall. In a rather formal procedure, the owner prepares his gong fu tea, a superior grade of oolong tea that requires special skills for processing. The tea has been blended and charcoal-fired at the shop. It is prepared on a draining tray set on a wooden table in the inner room. In an electric pot, charcoal-filtered water is brought to the correct temperature (195° to 210° for the semi-fermented oolongs). First the hot water is poured over the outside of a little clay teapot, then the heated pot is filled one-third full with the tea leaves and topped with water, which is immediately disposed of. This process washes the leaves. The pot is refilled, the leaves infused for thirty to forty-five seconds, and the tea poured into scenting cups and then into drinking cups. The brew is appraised in stages, first for color, then fragrance, then taste, and finally aftertaste, the most important part of tea drinking, which, according to tea expert Ip Wing Chi, owner of the shop, only comes with quality tea. The leaves are good for at least three more infusions, sometimes more. Tea is traditionally taken without food, but on occasion marbled tea eggs are served. These hard-boiled eggs are stewed in, among other ingredients, Ti Kuan Yin and other oolongs for flavor and Bolei for color. Ip Wing Chi respects tea because "it is a good supporting actor, so humble it never becomes the star at a meal, but makes it complete, enhancing it as it does poetry or music." He believes the philosophy and spirit of the Chinese people are reflected in their tea. On Sunday mornings, Chinese folk music harmonizes with the tea drinking at Tai Koon-Lock Cha, creating an *ah cha* (elegant gathering).

Lock Cha Tea Shop

Peak Café

China Club

STIR-FRIED NOODLES WITH SHIITAKE MUSHROOMS, SQUID, AND PORK

Makes 4 servings

8 ounces fresh Chinese egg noodles (mein) or fresh linguine

2 tablespoons plus 1 teaspoon peanut or vegetable oil

2 teaspoons finely minced ginger

2 teaspoons finely minced garlic

4 ounces Chinese-style barbecued pork or sugar-glazed baked ham, cut into $1/2$-inch-wide strips

4 ounces shiitake mushrooms, stems discarded, cut into $1/2$-inch-wide strips

1 small red bell pepper, cored, seeded, and chopped

$1/2$ cup sliced water chestnuts

4 ounces squid, cleaned and cut into $1/4$-inch-wide rings (8 ounces medium shrimp, peeled and deveined, or bay scallops may be substituted)

$2 1/2$ tablespoons soy sauce

1 teaspoon sugar

2 cups (8 ounces) fresh bean sprouts

1 medium carrot, shredded

2 tablespoons finely chopped shallots

Chopped scallions and whole cilantro leaves for garnish

In a large pot of boiling salted water, cook the noodles until barely tender, about 1 minute. Do not overcook. Drain, rinse under cold water, and drain again. Toss the noodles with the 1 teaspoon oil and set aside.

Heat a large skillet or wok over medium-high heat. Add the remaining 2 tablespoons oil and heat until the oil is very hot. Add the ginger and garlic and stir-fry until fragrant, about 30 seconds. Add the pork, shiitake mushrooms, bell pepper, and water chestnuts and stir-fry until the vegetables are heated through, about 2 minutes. Add the squid and stir-fry just until opaque, about 1 minute.

In a small bowl, mix the soy sauce and sugar. Add the cooked noodles to the wok and stir-fry for 1 minute. Add the soy sauce mixture, bean sprouts, and carrot. Stir-fry until well mixed, about 1 minute.

Transfer the noodles to serving bowls. Sprinkle with the shallots and garnish with scallions and cilantro.

MARBLED TEA EGGS

Makes 6 eggs

12 large eggs

1¹⁄₂ teaspoons coarse (kosher) salt, plus additional for serving

3 tablespoons loose Chinese black tea, such as Orange Pekoe

2 tablespoons soy sauce

2 star anise, broken into pieces

2 cinnamon sticks

Place the eggs in a saucepan. Pour in enough cold water to cover the eggs by 1 inch and add the salt. Bring to a simmer over medium heat and cook for 5 minutes.

Transfer the eggs to a bowl of cold water, reserving the cooking water in the saucepan. Let the eggs stand until cool enough to handle. Rap the shell of each egg all over with the back of a large spoon until the shell is covered with a web of cracks.

Add the tea leaves, soy sauce, star anise, and cinnamon to the water in the saucepan and bring to a boil over high heat. Reduce the heat to low. Carefully return the eggs to the saucepan, cover, and simmer gently until the egg shells have turned brown, about 2 hours. Remove from the heat. Cool the eggs in the liquid to room temperature. Cover the saucepan and refrigerate overnight. (The eggs will keep for up to 4 days, but will be best the first and second days.) Strain the steeping liquid through a fine sieve and reserve.

Peel the eggs and cut crosswise in half. Serve chilled, with small bowls of the cooking liquid and coarse salt.

Tea Zen, farther down Ladder Street, past the pavement vendors, and around the corner on Queens Road Central, is one of the oldest tea shops in Hong Kong. Operated by tea expert Ngan Ki Heung, the teahouse specializes in a variety of noble teas stored in tin canisters, which line the shelves along with whimsical Yixing teapots. Teas such as Bolei can be sampled at the counter. A fully fermented Bolei aged forty years or more is treated like a fine brandy. Bolei is a sophisticated tea, much favored by the Cantonese, and the proprietor advises drinking it after lunch to aid digestion and cut cholesterol. His Rosebud Tea, a black tea scented with roses, is recommended for slimming.

At the posh Fook Ming Tong tea shop in Prince's Building in Central Hong Kong, the tea tasted at the counter is brewed in water purified with volcanic rocks from Taiwan. The tea master for Fook Ming Tong travels to a number of China's tea gardens to select and buy the fifty varieties of teas stocked at the shop. Thomas Lee, founder and proprietor, insists it is not the number of teas that is important at Fook Ming Tong, but the quality and the care taken in preparation. He organizes tea-tasting competitions from time to time to promote tea appreciation.

Tucked into an antiquated building on an uphill street, the unpretentious Wing Kee Tea Merchants, a family business since 1855, still stores its teas in their original canisters and weighs the leaves in hand-held scales. This hole-in-the-wall shop is patronized by tea purists from all walks of life. Tasting Bolei tea at Wing Kee is serious business. The aged tea, dated 1952, is spooned into a zhong, topped with hot water, and poured out through a small opening into a tiny cup perched on a stack of similar cups. The first brew is discarded, leaving the cups heated. The leaves are covered with hot water again and the tea is ready to drink when the water remaining around the lid of the zhong has evaporated. The clarity is checked—transparency is essential to good tea. Then, the clear nut-brown tea is poured into the tiny cups. The proprietor forms his mouth into a pouch, lets the tea fall onto his gums, and declares the taste is like velvet.

daily tea

A TEA MERCHANT'S TEA

High on a windy hill overlooking Repulse Bay, Thomas Lee has set aside a corner in his house for tea drinking. He is the founder and owner of the Fook Ming Tong tea shops and takes the tea ritual seriously. A dark wood table holds a tea boat, clay teapot, porcelain cups, and a few other utensils crucial to tea preparation in the gong fu style. This is the method used traditionally in brewing Ti Kuan Yin, an oolong tea, to bring out its mellow flavor and aroma. The small teapot is filled half to two-thirds full with the leaves, which are steeped for thirty to forty-five seconds in just enough water to fill four tiny cups for one round of tea. Ti Kuan Yin is also called Monkey Plucked, as the finest grade comes from the tops of trees grown in the mountain recesses of Fujian, and tradition holds that monkeys were once used to pluck the leaves. It was only after starting his tea shops that Thomas discovered that his ancestors had been in the tea business in Fujian during the Sung dynasty. They probably would have remained so had not one of them, a concubine, displeased the emperor. As punishment, the emperor sentenced all of her family members to death. Luckily, they had advance warning and fled more quickly than it takes to brew a pot of oolong tea.

A MANDARIN AFTERNOON TEA

Alan Chan, creative director of Alan Chan Design Company, is a serious collector of distinctive tea equipment. His exquisite eighteenth-century export silver tea service is set on an ebony mah jongg table in front of stained glass doors brought from Shanghai, once the glamour capital of the world and major port of call of the tea trade in its golden age, in the early part of the twentieth century. The cosmopolitan urban sprawl, with its Anglo-Indian architecture, was a lure to foreign entrepreneurs and adventurers, who were seduced by its fast-paced life, grand hotels, and private clubs on Nanjing Road. In Shanghai style, Alan serves sweet and salty bites at afternoon tea along with the delicate Pingsuey, a black tea from Zhejiang Province, a little south of the city. This is the same area where Long Jing tea is produced, another Shanghai favorite. Festive celebration cakes served at Mandarin weddings share the tea table with a mythical Chinese animal that ensures good luck. The design of Alan's bone china tea service was inspired by Chinese poetry written by a Tang poet and presented in calligraphy.

AN AUTUMN TEA

In China, the Mid-Autumn or Autumn Moon Festival is celebrated with mooncakes, which are traditionally exchanged as gifts to express wishes for a happy autumn and mild winter. Square or round, these sweet biscuitlike cakes are filled with a sweet puree of red beans or lotus seeds.

White is the color of choice for teacups as it best complements the tea color. Lu Yu, in his tea classic, the *Ch'a Ching*, considered the blue glaze of northern China the ideal color for tea as it lent additional greenness to the beverage, while white made it look pinkish and distasteful. He, however, was brewing cake tea. Later, the Sung tea masters prepared their powdered tea in blue, black, and dark brown bowls, colors that enhanced the appearance of their whipped tea. The Ming steeped their pale-colored tea in white porcelain.

It is not unusual for caged songbirds to be brought to tea. At Wan Loy Teahouse on Shanghai Street in Hong Kong, patrons brought their birds there in bamboo cages and hung them on special poles so their songs could be appreciated by all. Wan Loy is now a memory because of the continual modernization of Hong Kong, but in China, "bird teahouses" still exist.

AN AMERICAN IN HONG KONG

Sally Harpole, a lawyer who practices in Asia, lived in mainland China for a number of years and now lives in Hong Kong. She speaks fluent Mandarin, is a collector of Chinese art and antiques, and is a tea lover. She learned early on that tea and Yixing pottery go hand in hand—that the clay pottery enhances the enjoyment of the brew—and over the years has accumulated fine early-twentieth-century Yixingware. Clay from Yixing, a city near Shanghai, varies in color from black and dark green to brown and terra-cotta. Tea connoisseurs keep a separate teapot for each tea to ensure that the flavors and scents remain consistent and untainted. Sally's favorite tea is Yin Hao Jasmine, not only one of the most expensive teas but also the tea of choice of James Bond. Yin Hao Jasmine, a scented green tea, is grown in Fujian. The tea leaves are picked in spring, then steamed and stored until late summer when jasmine is in bloom. Jasmine buds are picked at midday and in the evening, when they are open, then mixed with the tea leaves in machines that control the temperature and humidity. The jasmine fragrance is absorbed into the tea leaves in four hours. To make the higher grades of the Yin Hao Jasmine, this flavoring process is repeated four or five times within a month.

Sally's tea table includes her sextagonal stoneware tea caddies and handle-less blue-and-white Jingdezhen-patterned teacups. The ancient town of Jingdezhen is the site of one of China's oldest and most famous traditional kilns.

China TEAS

"What tongue can tell the various kinds of tea?
Of Blacks and Greens, of Hyson and Bohea,
With simple Congou, Pekoe, and Souchong,
Cowslip the fragrant, Gunpowder the strong?"

ANONYMOUS

China produces green, white, oolong, and black teas in the provinces of Zhejiang, Hunan, Anhui, Sichuan, Fujian, and Yunnan. Some tea is still cultivated on farms in small quantities as it always has been, but since China became a Communist state, the major supply comes from state tea communes.

GREEN TEAS

Freshness is imperative to green teas and they should be used within one hundred days of plucking. They are taken without milk, sugar, or lemon.

Pi Lo Chun The most delicate and rare of China's greens, brews to a pale yellow green in the cup, sweet aroma and rounded body. A connoisseur's tea.

Long Jing (Dragon Well) Pale gold in the cup, slightly vegetative aroma and taste. A refined tea.

Pinhead Gunpowder (Pearl Tea) Leaves rolled to small pellets. Brews to pale amber and has a pleasant, mildly bitter taste.

Young Hyson A slightly sweet tea of excellent quality.

WHITE TEAS

Slightly fermented teas produced only in China. the whites are the least processed. between green and oolong. They are taken without milk. sugar. or lemon.

Silvery Tip Pekoe Most costly of the white teas. rare even in China. Leaves are silver. Brews to pale gold and has a sweetish. mellow flavor.

Pai Mu Tan (White Peony) Made from a mix of two white tea plants. Has a flowery aroma.

OOLONG TEAS

Semi-fermented teas. They are taken without milk. sugar. or lemon.

Ti Kuan Yin (Monkey Tea) Brews to amber and has a subtle, earthy flavor.

Fancy Formosa Oolong A bright tea with a subtle peachy flavor.

CONGOU TEAS

(China Black Teas) Referred to as red teas in China. Most can be taken with milk. sugar. or lemon. Congous from South China are referred to as China's clarets: those from the north as China's burgundies.

Keemun A slightly sweet. full-bodied tea with a rich aroma. China's finest congou. Until a hundred years ago. it was an ordinary green tea. One explanation of the change to black is told in the story of a bureaucrat who. upon being fired from his position. moved away to a black tea–producing area. There he learned tea cultivation. and later returned to the Keemun area in Anhui Province to apply his knowledge. The result. the birth of a superb black tea from what was an ordinary green.

Winey Keemun Excellent breakfast tea. Full-bodied. mellow flavor.

Pingsuey Mild. well-rounded tea.

Yunnan Large-leafed tea. Rich. slightly sweet.

Ching Wo The coppery-colored Ching Wo. from Fujian Province. is a delicate tea with excellent body and aroma.

SCENTED TEAS

Jasmine Green or oolong teas scented with jasmine blossoms. Fragrant and delicate. Taken without milk, sugar, or lemon.

Rose Black tea scented with rose blossoms.

Lychee Sweet black tea scented with lychee fruit.

Lapsang souchong Black tea smoked over fresh pine logs. Rich, tarry flavor. Can take milk and sugar.

COMPRESSED TEA

Pu Erh A green tea fermented by introducing bacteria into the leaves, which are then aged twenty to sixty years. Aroma of damp soil and an earthy flavor. Chestnut color in the cup.

brewing tea the chinese way

Fine China tea should be infused in a small clay teapot or porcelain *zhong* (covered cup) to get the most flavor. Traditionally, thimble-sized cups are used. The water should be as pure as possible. Spring water is the ideal. In China, tea is brewed in water from the spring nearest the tea garden.

Fill a small clay teapot or zhong one-third to one-half full with tea leaves. Heat water to a boil, then let cool 110 to 160 degrees for green tea, 175 to 195 degrees for white, 195 to 210 degrees for semi-fermented, 210 degrees for black.

Fill the teapot one-quarter full with water at the recommended temperature, and immediately pour it out. This washes the leaves, starts the leaves opening, and heats the pot.

Refill the pot with water at the same temperature. Infuse for one to five minutes for green tea, one to two minutes for white tea, and fifteen seconds to one minute for semi-fermented or black tea.

Pour the entire contents of the pot into cups. Green and white teas may be infused two or three more times, semi-fermented and black teas five or more times. A slightly longer steeping time is necessary for these additional infusions.

practical uses of tea in china

"The effect of tea is cooling. As a drink, it suits very well persons of self-restraint and good conduct. When feeling hot, thirsty, depressed, suffering from headache, eye-ache, fatigue of the four limbs, or pains in the joints, one should drink tea only, four or five times."

LU YU, CH'A CHING, 780

- To absorb odors in the refrigerator, fill a small open container with dried used tea leaves.
- To keep shoes fresh, fill eight-inch squares of muslin with dried tea leaves, tie into bags, and place inside the shoes overnight to absorb odors.
- To clean pots and pans, fill eight-inch squares of muslin with wet or dried used tea leaves, tie into bags, and use for scrubbing.
- To flavor chicken soup, use oolong tea instead of water for boiling the chicken.
- To relieve headache, use a pillow stuffed with dried used tea leaves.
- To remove tea stains, apply dishwashing powder to damp stain, leave 10 minutes, soak in a small amount of water for an additional few minutes, rub stain area gently, and rinse.

storing tea

To protect tea from its enemies—air, light, heat, and humidity—store the leaves in an airtight tin, tin-lined box, or opaque ceramic pot. Green teas should be used as soon as possible, as the fresher the leaves, the more flavor. But properly stored, they can keep up to six months. White and oolong teas will keep up to a year, and black teas more than a year. As a rule, Pu Erh is better the longer it is kept.

the tea caravan trade

"THEY TAKE A TEA-CUP HALF-FILLED WITH boiling water; to that they add some pinches of tsampa, and then mix those materials into a sort of wretched paste, neither cooked nor uncooked, not hot, nor cold, which is then swallowed and is considered breakfast, dinner, or supper as the case may be." PÈRE ÉVARIST RÉGIS HUC, *SOUVENIRS D'UN VOYAGE DANS LA TARTARIE, LE TIBET, ET LA CHINE,* 1848

Tea Routes from China

THE EXPORT OF TEA to the world from China began during the Sung dynasty. Bricks and bales of compressed tea harnessed on the backs of mules, yaks, horses, camels, and coolies were hauled across arid desert and scrublands from northern China into Mongolia, and over steep, craggy mountain passes into Tibet from Sichuan and Yunnan. The hearty hot beverage brewed from the shavings of the brick tea warmed the Mongolian nomads and fabled people of the Tibetan mountains in the cold winters, but, more importantly, the tea substituted as a vegetable, crucial to their diets. Both have a unique way of preparing tea, which they practice to this day.

The Mongolians brew yak butterfat with their tea, strain it, and mix it with

Tibetan tea bricks

milk, butter, and roasted grain. The Tibetans steep shavings from their crushed tea bricks in water overnight. The next day, in a *jhandong* (churn), they churn the tea with salt, milk, and yak butter into a thick, oily drink, more like the consistency of hot chocolate than tea. The hearty tea is ordinarily served in simple bowls, but on special occasions, upper-class Tibetans set a regal tea table with porcelain, gold, and silver. The buttered tea is transferred from the wooden jhandong into a silver teapot, kept hot on a charcoal-filled copper and silver *maypo*, and poured into ornate his and hers porcelain cups perched on gold and silver stands.

Mongolian and Tibetan coins were of little value to the Chinese, so they exchanged compressed tea cakes and, later, brick tea for wool, furs, skins, and horses from the Mongolians and wool, musk, and medicines from the Tibetans. The tea bricks were marked off so change could be made, and their value increased depending on the distance of the journey from the tea garden to its destination. This practice ceased only at the beginning of the twentieth century. Tea bricks are still produced in China, but they make better ornaments than a satisfying brew.

Russia initially passed up the tea habit despite early acquaintance with the beverage. Two Cossacks first brought news of the Chinese drink in 1567, then in 1618, the Chinese embassy presented a gift of tea to Czar Alexis in Moscow. And the first ambassador to the court of the Mogul emperor of India declined a gift of tea to Czar Michael Romanov, because although he himself had experienced the brew, he did not believe the czar would take to it. Tea finally got a foothold in Russia in 1689, when Russia and China signed the

Nerchinsk Treaty, establishing a boundary and a single trade route. Curiously, two Jesuits, a Portuguese and a Frenchman, drew up the treaty. Jesuits were allowed to live in the Chinese court at the time, as long as they kept their religious beliefs to themselves. They served as interpreters to the Manchu emperor and enlightened him with valuable information on Western culture and taste. For the entrepreneurial Chinese, this knowledge would blossom into the enormous export trade of the seventeenth and eighteenth centuries.

The Chinese, preferring to keep foreigners at arm's length, insisted that trade be confined to Usk Kayakhta, a bleak outpost deep in the hinterlands, a thousand miles from Peking and three thousand miles from Moscow. Horses and mules hauled the tea on the first leg of the journey from Tientsin, clambering over hazardous mountain terrain to Kalgan, two hundred miles northeast of Peking. At Kalgan the tea was loaded on two to three hundred camels, each carrying six hundred pounds, and at a plodding but steady pace of two and a half miles an hour, averaging about twenty-five miles a day, they lumbered across eight hundred miles of the barren Gobi Desert before finally reaching Usk Kayakhta. There the Russians, who had driven their camels through Siberia and Mongolia, would unload the furs, load the chests of tea, and start the return journey, which could take up to a year. The still-scarce tea was a luxury in Russia and only the aristocrats could pay the fifteen rubles per pound. Prices eased off when Czarina Elizabeth started a private caravan trade in 1735, which increased the supply, but tea was only made affordable to most Russians with the opening of the Siberian Railway in 1880. An arduous journey that once took up to a year and more was cut down to seven weeks, and the colorful camel caravans and Usk Kayakhta lost their relevance.

The Russians became quick devotees of the China drink made in their unique samovar, a metal urn with a spigot and an internal tube for heating water. The samovar may have originated in China, as one historian noted on seeing a similar-looking vessel used to heat punch in Canton in the early seventeenth century. Black or green tea is steeped in a teapot and placed on top of the steaming samovar. When the brew is strong, one quarter of a glass or teacup is filled with tea into which boiling water is added from the samovar, diluting the beverage to the desired strength. Some sip their tea through a sugar cube held between the teeth, some stir a spoonful of jam into it, others take it with lemon. Tea is grown in Georgia above the Black Sea and in Azerbaijan near the Caspian Sea, but the production is hardly enough to satisfy Russia's thirst for the brew, and teas from China, Taiwan, India, and Sri

Lanka are imported. Russian Blend, Russian Caravan, Czar Alexander, and other such romantic names are blends of imported teas, slightly smoked or flavored with citrus fruits and bergamot.

Simultaneously with the Russian trade, China tea traveled farther west on the northern caravan route, branching off southwest along the famous silk route through Mongolia and Turkestan to Afghanistan and on through the Arab countries to Egypt. Arab merchants were among the early travelers to China and it was one such adventurer from Persia (Iran) who brought the first news of China tea to Europe, as recounted in Giovanni Battista Ramusio's *The Tale of Hajji Mahommed*, published in Venice in 1559. Later, in *Navigatione et Viaggi*, Ramusio wrote, "And it is so highly valued and esteemed that everyone going on a journey takes it with him, and those people would gladly give a sack of rhubarb for one ounce of Chai Catai. . . ."

During the eighteenth and nineteenth centuries, orientalists painted exotic imageries of tea in daily life in the Middle East. Canvases portray bejeweled Arab women seated on paisley or geometric-patterned carpets, wrapped head to toe in rich fabrics, pouring tea from rounded silver teapots into glasses set on brass trays. They painted Moorish cafés filled with amicable tea drinkers

lounging on banquettes or sitting cross-legged on floor mats, camel drivers huddled around fires in arid landscapes clutching bowls of tea, and merchants at roadside samovar stands in bleached villages drinking cups of sugary green and black teas served by turbaned boys.

Afghans and Iranians, like the Russians, use the samovar. In Afghanistan, black tea is drunk for warmth, while green tea seasoned with a pinch of cardamom and served with sugar on the side is taken to quench thirst. Primary-colored floral teapots and handleless porcelain teacups stand in rows on the shelves at tea stands and in tearooms, ready for tea enthusiasts. Iranians easily consume seven or eight cups of tea a day.

The Turks were bartering for tea on the Mongolian border of China as early as 475. Their tea is made in two nested pots, called a *cay danlik*. The bottom pot boils the water while the top one is used for brewing. Strong black tea is kept hot all day in Turkish homes and the brew is diluted with water as desired. Glasses are filled to the quarter mark with tea from a silver teapot into which hot water has been added. Proper tea making, *demlikacay*, is so crucial in a Turkish home that a mother will take particular notice of the brewing capabilities of her son's intended bride. Nut-filled sweets traditionally accompany tea in Turkey.

Oddly, teahouses are called coffeehouses in Iraq, but despite the name, they are strictly teahouses. Iraq produces some tea which is blended with Ceylon tea. The brew is steeped in a metal teapot, transferred to a smaller pot, and served in tiny glasses set on a tray. Black tea is the norm, but *nome basra*, a sweet fruit tea made from dried lemon, is popular as well. Both are served with small pastries filled with dates or nuts. There is a great demand for herbal teas in Iraq today to make up for the lack of medicines that has resulted from trade sanctions. Chamomile is taken to sooth the stomach, and a brew of dried wild "blue flower" tempers headaches and the discomforts of a cold.

Egypt has a boundless enthusiasm for tea, dating back to the Sultan's court in the fifteenth century. Tea is as important as bread, sugar, and oil and despite the cost, the government insures that everyone can afford it. Egyptians drink strong Indian and Ceylon teas with plenty of sugar and no milk. In their tearooms, tea is served in glasses, with sugar, a glass of cold water on the side, and, sometimes, a glass of mint for those with a taste for the sweet mint tea so common in Morocco.

The caravan trade route marked on ancient atlases was long ago, but it remains one of the most romantic and picturesque chapters of the tea trade and brought China's tea culture farther west.

RUSSIAN TEA ROOM SPICE CAKE

Makes 8 servings

$^1/_2$ cup ($2^1/_2$ ounces) dried
   cranberries

$^1/_2$ pound (2 sticks) plus
   4 tablespoons unsalted butter,
   at room temperature

$^1/_2$ cup walnuts, very finely
   chopped

$2^1/_4$ cups cake flour

$^1/_2$ teaspoon baking powder

$^1/_4$ teaspoon baking soda

1 teaspoon ground cinnamon

1 teaspoon grated nutmeg

$^1/_2$ teaspoon ground cloves

$^1/_2$ teaspoon salt

$^3/_4$ cup buttermilk

2 tablespoons dark rum

$1^1/_2$ cups granulated sugar

4 large egg yolks

2 cups confectioners' sugar

2 teaspoons ground ginger

Approximately 3 tablespoons
   water

APPLE KISSEL

1 cup water

3 tablespoons sugar

5 medium Golden Delicious apples,
   peeled, cored, and cut
   into eighths

1 tablespoon fresh lemon juice

Sweetened whipped cream for serving
   (optional)

In a small bowl, soak the cranberries in hot water to cover until plump, about 30 minutes.

Position a rack in the center of the oven and preheat the oven to 350°F. Coat the inside of a 10-inch tube pan with 2 tablespoons of the butter. Sprinkle the chopped walnuts inside the pan, turning the pan to coat.

Sift the flour, baking powder, baking soda, cinnamon, nutmeg, cloves, and salt onto a piece of waxed paper. Sift two more times and set aside. In a measuring cup, mix the buttermilk and rum. Drain the cranberries and pat dry with paper towels.

In the bowl of an electric mixer, beat the remaining $1/2$ pound (2 sticks) plus 2 tablespoons butter and the granulated sugar at high speed, until light in color, about 5 minutes. One at a time, beat in the egg yolks. Starting with the buttermilk, add buttermilk mixture and the dry ingredients, one third at a time, beating well after each addition, and scraping down the sides of the bowl with a rubber spatula as needed. Fold in the cranberries. Pour into the prepared pan and smooth the top.

Bake until a toothpick inserted in the center of the cake comes out clean, 45 to 55 minutes. Remove from the oven and cool on a wire cake rack for 5 minutes. (Leave the oven on.)

Sift the confectioners' sugar and ginger into a medium bowl. Gradually stir in enough water to make a thick, pourable syrup.

Run a knife around the inside of the pan and unmold the cake onto the rack. Turn the cake right side up. Place the rack on a baking sheet. Pour the glaze over the hot cake, smoothing it over the top and sides with a metal cake spatula. Use the spatula to pick up the glaze on the baking sheet and spread over any bare spots on the cake. With the cake still on the rack over the baking sheet, bake until the glaze is firm and shiny, 1 to 2 minutes. Remove from the oven and cool.

Prepare the apple kissel: In a medium saucepan, bring the water and sugar to a boil. Add the apples and lemon juice and stir well. Reduce the heat and simmer until the apples are tender, about 10 minutes. Cool slightly.

Use a wide spatula to transfer the cake to a serving platter. Arrange some of the apples in a decorative pattern on top of the cake, and pour the remaining apples into the hole in the center of the cake. Serve warm or at room temperature, with whipped cream, if desired.

japan

"IN THE TEA-ROOM THE FEAR OF REPETI-
tion is a constant presence. . . . If you have a living
flower, a painting of flowers is not allowable. If you
are using a round kettle, the water pitcher should
be angular. A cup with a black glaze should not
be associated with a tea-caddy of black lacquer."

KAKUZO OKAKURA, *THE BOOK OF TEA*

THE JAPANESE NEVER BELIEVED the Shen Nung legend of the discovery of tea. To them, the secrets of tea were brought to China in 519 by the Indian saint Bodhidharma, or Daruma as he was known in Japan, the founder of the Zen sect of Buddhism (from dhyāna, the Sanskrit word for meditation).

Japan learned of the Tang brick tea through the Buddhist monks around 593, not long after it was used in China, but it was not until 805, when a Japanese Buddhist, Dengyo Daishi, who had been studying in China, brought home some tea seeds that planting began. The emperor Saga (810–823), on sampling the brew from the first harvest, was so taken by it that he ordered planting in five provinces near the capital and declared tea the beverage of the court. The "Drink of Ceremony" was prepared as Lu Yu advised, sipped between sessions of poetry reading and given all the respect it commanded in China.

All things Chinese, the arts, literature, ceremonies, and aesthetic pastimes, were fashionable with the Japanese at this time. They adopted the culture hungrily, out of pure responsive appreciation, making copies of Chinese paintings and porcelains more exquisite than the originals. The Japanese could never simply be idolaters, given their intuitive creative skills and fine taste, the genius of which is reflected in their own art. The enthusiasm for tea lasted until Saga's death; then it declined, partly because of civil strife in Japan and political upheavals in China, which resulted in a break between the two countries. Tea languished in shadowy limbo for about three hundred years except in the Buddhist temples, where it was part of a religious ritual and aided in keeping the monks alert during lengthy periods of meditation.

After the long hiatus, it was a Buddhist once more, the priest Eisai (1141–1215), who, upon his return from his studies at the great Zen monasteries in China, reintroduced tea cultivation in Japan. Part of Abbot Eisai's garden in Reisen-ji Temple in Hizen Province still remains, and cuttings from his original plants are the source of most of the tea gardens in Japan.

Abbot Eisai wrote the first tea book in Japan. *The Book of Tea Sanitation*, a health book published in 1191. He once demonstrated the powers of tea when called to the bedside of a dying samurai. Actually the illness was only a case of too much alcohol, for which he prescribed the Sung powdered tea and left his patient a copy of his tea book. When news of the samurai's "miraculous recovery" spread, tea was acclaimed as a miracle beverage. In time it became so popular that vendors began to sell it outside the temple gates. The success of the hawkers inspired entrepreneurs to open shops to serve the brew, the first tearooms in Japan.

Japan was fortunate to have been able to resist the Mongol invasion in 1281 and to sustain the great Sung culture that was so disastrously devasted in China. Samurai warriors and Buddhist monks preserved the Sung tea tradition each in their own way. The samurai held lively tea tournaments (*cha-yoria*) in elaborate, two-storied tea pavilions. Tasters sat before the image of Buddha and sampled teas to see who could tell the true tea, that grown in Togano-o Kozan-ji Temple, from the hundreds of varieties grown elsewhere. There was music and entertainment to amuse the guests and plenty of sake, the fermented rice drink. The tournaments inevitably degenerated into showy displays of wealth, raucous behavior, and gambling, an unfortunate departure from their original intent. Some shoguns banned the contests, but the tournaments continued up to the early part of the twentieth century.

The Buddhists were bound to tea by an intrinsic philosophic relationship with the drink. The Zen followers drank powdered tea from a communal bowl before an image of Bodhidharma. This solemn rite eventually led to the development of the tea ceremony, *chanoyu*, in the fifteenth century, a religious art form in which tea becomes the vehicle of its philosophic ideals. The ritual demands the smallest action be performed to absolute perfection, a solemn observance of measured gestures performed with precise rules in a

carefully thought out ambience. "Not a color to disturb the tone of the room, not a sound to mar the rhythm of things, not a gesture to obtrude the harmony, not a word to break the unity of the surroundings, all movements to be performed simply and naturally—such were the aims of the tea ceremony," as described by Kakuzo Okakura in *The Book of Tea*.

The tea ceremony influenced all of Japan's fine arts, including garden design, flower arrangement, architecture, calligraphy, painting, lacquer, and ceramic arts. The tea ceremony as it is performed today owes much to Zen tea master Sen Rikyu (1522–1591), who amended it in the sixteenth century. The ritual is less tedious and elaborate than it once was, with the focus on purity and serenity. Sen Rikyu emphasized the aesthetics of the ceremony, incorporating nature, architecture, and art, and advocated consideration and politeness. He remarked, "In Zen, truth is pursued through discipline of meditation in order to realize enlightenment, while in Tea we use training in the actual procedures of making tea to achieve the same end."

The Japanese knew tea in all its stages, the brick of the Tang, powder of the Sung, and leaf of the Ming, but it was the powdered green tea of the Sung that captivated their palates and is dearest to their hearts. For general consumption, however, the leaf green teas are the daily brews and have been since the seventeenth century. The most exclusive green teas in Japan are produced in Uji, on the plains where the pH factor and water are good. Other areas such as Shizuoka and Kyushu are important tea areas too, but Uji has the lead on growing the most select teas, some of the best produced from plants grown from cuttings of Eisai's tea bushes at Reisen-ji Temple garden that were planted in the twelfth century. The most prized Uji tea is Gyokuro. It is hand-produced, unlike most of Japan's greens, which are made by ingenious quality-maintaining machines. In the case of Gyokuro, the bushes are shaded with straw matting for three weeks before plucking, to increase the amount of caffeine and decrease the tannin content. After steaming, which prevents the oxidation necessary to produce oolong and black teas, the leaves are basket-fired in five-pound quantities and rolled, producing needlelike leaves.

Tea is so omnipresent in Japanese culture that scholars cannot help speaking of the "divine elixir" as part of their civilization. An old story tells of a Buddhist monk who, on explaining reincarnation, smashes a cup of green tea against the edge of a table. The cup shatters; its fragments, tea and all, spill to the floor. "You see," the teacher points out, "the cup is no longer a cup, but the tea will always be tea." The way of tea sets the standards of conduct for an ethical and moral life in Japan, and a man who possesses these ideals is said to be a man with "tea in him."

Tea in Japan

"Like visual musicians, the Japanese seem to have perfect pitch in areas of shape and color."

TRUMAN CAPOTE, *THE DOGS BARK*

tea in tearooms and sweetshops

To take *cha* (tea) in Japan is to drink *ocha* (green tea) with *wagashi*, the exquisite miniature confections made of bean paste, rice powder, sugar, and green tea. They balance the slightly bitter taste of green tea. Creating harmony with opposites is an important aspect of Japanese culture. Like flowers, the sweets change with the seasons, indulging the senses of sight, scent, flavor, and touch. Their lyrical names, *matsu no yuki*, *wakaba kage*, *hanagoromo*, appeal to the sense of sound. In varying shapes inspired by literature, paintings, textiles, and elements of nature, they are similar to marzipan.

Toraya, the oldest traditional confectioner in Japan, said to date back to the Nara Period (eighth century), supplied wagashi to the imperial family in the sixteenth century as it still does today. The business is now run by the seventeenth generation of the original family. Neatly displayed under glass at all the Toraya establishments, which include tearooms, the whimsical wagashi are shaped and colored to resemble seasonal happenings. A peach blossom celebrates spring, a dewdrop on a leaf or a tiny fish floating in a transparent cube has summer inferences, a red and yellow fan-shaped sweet mirrors a ginkgo leaf in autumn. In honor of Boys' Day, a parsnip-shaped wagashi wishes a boy to grow tall.

In the spring, at Kikuya, in Tokyo, azuki and white bean paste wagashi are formed into sweet pastel flowers. Twenty varieties of wagashi have been made by hand each day here for sixty years, the amount needed for sale gauged as the day goes along. Sometimes in the warm season, wagashi is replaced by *uji-kori*: green tea syrup drizzled over shaved ice, which is eaten with sweet azuki beans.

Tea Leaves at Matsuya department store is a little tea oasis designed to counteract the busy, hectic life in modern Tokyo. Water splashes gently in a corner, and a delicate tree arches over the tea counter, bringing nature together with tea drinking. On a summer day, a cool palette is created with iced Matcha, a powdered green tea, and wagashi in leaf form, made of green tea and rice powder with a red bean paste filling.

Rice cakes called *mochi* make intriguing tea bites too. Matsuzaki, a tea-room and rice shop, has been making wagashi, mochi, and *chimaki*, sweetened rice wrapped in bamboo leaves, for one hundred and ninety years. Teatime at Matsuzaki consists of a healthy combination of sweetened rice, bean paste confections, and green tea.

Ippodo Tea Company, the finest tea shop in Kyoto, has been in business since 1717. The shelves are lined with vintage tea boxes and ceramic storage jars that house the earthy green teas of Japan. Sencha, which when brewed has a perfect blend of sweetness and sharpness, is most in demand, with Iribancha and Genmaicha close seconds. The former is a roasted green tea, the latter a green tea sprinkled with toasted popped rice, giving the brew a faint popcorn flavor. There is a small tea-tasting room at Ippodo where other teas, such as Gyokuro, Houjicha, and Matcha, can be sampled.

Tea shops in Japan celebrate the first spring tea harvest with the same eager excitement and fanfare that greet the arrival of the season's first Beaujolais Nouveau in France. In the seventeenth and eighteenth centuries, nine great jars holding samples of the first teas of the season, accompanied by guards and attendants from Uji, were paraded in a spectacular three-hundred-mile pageant to the shogun in Tokyo. The procession was welcomed and feasted in each fief along the way, and even the highest nobles who met the cortège were required to prostrate themselves before the venerable jars.

the way of tea

"Make a delicious bowl of tea; lay the charcoal so that it heats the water; arrange the flowers as they are in the field; in summer suggest coolness, in winter, warmth; do everything ahead of time; prepare for rain; and give those with whom you find yourself every consideration."

SEN RIKYU (1522–1591)

A TEA MASTER'S TEA

John McGee, a tea master for the Urasenke Foundation, was first introduced to the tea ceremony as a young man, when he discovered a traditional tea-house in a Japanese tea garden while working at the Osaka World's Fair in 1970. He was intrigued and returned often to the teahouse, always finding something new in the tea ceremony. It appealed to his intellect, heart, and soul, satisfying his love of art and pottery, combining the spiritual and philosophical aspects of life. He moved to Japan and began studying with grand tea master Soshitsu Sen XV. Seven years later, he was allowed to become a teacher. He continued his studies, which included Buddhist philosophy, cooking, interiors, and gardening, essentials to becoming a tea master, for ten years. John's daily life is completely influenced by the Way of Tea. He lives in a seventeenth-century farmhouse outside Kyoto, surrounded by gardens, rice paddies, and mountains. In the most formal room of his historic one-storied, thatch-roofed house, John performs the tea ceremony on a tatami mat. Purple wildflowers to reflect the countryside are arranged in the *tokonoma*, the place of honor in a Japanese room, the kettle is on the fire, and the implements are laid out in a precise, prescribed order: drinking bowl, tea scoop, whisk, cleaning cloth, powdered tea. The tea is from the May picking of a one-hundred-year-old tea bush. With mesmerizing motions and the deftness of a master, John heats the bowl with hot water from the steaming kettle, discards it, puts two tea scoops of tea in the heated bowl, adds not quite a scoopful of hot water, whisks it to a froth, rotates the bowl and then presents it with both hands to his guest, who has already been served a sweet. The required utensils and movements are a constant, but the interaction between host and guest creates the variables that make each ceremony unique.

A complete tea ceremony takes several hours, with time allotted for the guests to appreciate the ambience of the tea room and enjoy the beauty of the fire, the utensils, and the scroll that expresses the mood the tea master wishes to set. The scroll may be a painting, a poem, or a meaningful Zen thought penned in calligraphy. A couple of hours are spent eating and drinking sake, demonstrating the host's cooking skills. After the first tea, the guests are invited outside to enjoy nature, to admire the garden or a sunset, while the host replaces the scroll with a significant flower arrangement. A series of gongs, one loud, one soft, one loud, one soft, two medium, and a final loud one, summons the guests back to the tea room to share the frothy green Matcha from one bowl. The shorter ceremony is simply a bowl of the powdered tea properly prepared and presented, preceded by a sweet.

John is a man with "tea in him." He is a collector of fine Japanese antiques and lives among them in traditional Japanese style. His spring fireside tea for two has the simplicity of the tea ceremony. At the *irori* (fireside), he has made patterns in the sand surrounding the fire, which is set in front of a *shoji*, the sliding paper door dividing the room from the kitchen beyond. The irori is at the center of the house, at an equal distance from all the other rooms. Water heats in the sixteenth-century iron kettle over the fire. The tea is stored in a vine-painted caddy to be whisked in a black pottery *chawan* (teabowl). A sweet wrapped in an oak leaf celebrates the month of May. The fire, utensils, tea, sweet—everything pleases the eye. In keeping with the antique setting, the cushions are covered in old sake-straining fabric aged to a leather look.

A *chabako* (tea box), holding all the elements for an informal tea, can be carried anywhere at a moment's notice. John's courtyard contemplation garden is a serene atmosphere for a summer chabako in the country. In town, he favors his upstairs tea room, an oasis with only the sound of wind in the trees to intrude on the silence. The chabako contains a tea caddy, bamboo tea scoop, whisk, purple wiping cloth (the imperial color indicates a male host), hydrangea teabowl, and a porcelain container holding little sweets. Everything has been carefully selected to set a summer mood. Host and guest will drink the thick Matcha tea from the same bowl, creating a sense of oneness. Thick Matcha is made from a different tea leaf than thin Matcha, which is prepared with more water per cup.

A CERAMIST'S TEA

Sen Rikyu's ritual for chanoyu had a great influence on the development of Japanese pottery, as it required a small jar to hold the powdered tea, a drinking bowl, washbowl, cake dish, water container, incense box, incense burner, fire holder, and vase to hold flowers. Rikyu favored simple native pottery, and by the end of the sixteenth century, potters and tea masters too were producing ceremonial teaware, which became highly collectible.

Seimei Tsuji is one of Japan's celebrated ceramists and a devotee of the ceremony. He and his wife live on the outskirts of Tokyo, where he built a teahouse. It is reached after passing through a small wooden gate and following a *roji* (stone path) that winds through a verdant setting. On warm days the path is sprinkled with water, creating a dewy, cool ground. The simple teahouse was designed to allow it to bask in sunlight during the day and to capture the red glow of Japanese maples in the autumn. Candles are used at night.

Seimei has used ancient woods he collected all over Japan to craft the teahouse, which consists of two rooms: one a narrow tea-preparation room, which holds the tea utensils, the other where guests and host take tea. The walls are prepared with old *tatan*, a mixture of straw and special clay, and covered in Japanese paper tinted with squid ink in shades from deep aubergine at the base to camel at the top. To set a seasonal mood in the tokonoma, a scroll painting of ducks in a pond hangs on the wall and spring wildflowers are arranged in a ceramic vase. Guests must enter by crawling through a small opening, submitting all to the same humble status. Seimei uses his own crafted pottery bowl for the tea but first presents *yakimanjyu* in a red lacquer bowl. The classic baked sweet bean paste confection is from Ise, a place known for traditional sweets, in southern Japan.

The Tsujis are in harmony with their surroundings, and their culture imbues their daily lives. On cool days, they take tea by the irori in their house. They buy the freshest green tea and brew it in spring water from Mount Miwayama in Nara in a teapot made in Ise. Woody incense cleanses the air and encourages relaxation. On warm days, they take their tea outdoors in the sylvan setting of an eight-hundred-year-old stone basin. The teapot is Bizen, named for its place of origin in western Japan.

Seimei's studio is on the second floor of the house. He prepares lectures, paints, and takes tea here. He keeps his treasured ceramics collection in this light, airy room, some tied up with ribbon in their original boxes.

WEST MEETS EAST

Jurgen Lehl started his career in France, but he has been living and designing textiles, clothing, and home furnishings in Japan for many years. The culture, aesthetics, and discipline of his adopted home suit his spartan nature and artistic temperament. He collects ceramics and crafts, which he uses in his showroom to serve Kukicha, a low-caffeine brew of roasted leaves and twigs from the tea plant. Every morning, he drinks a special tea of roasted sesame seeds, which promises shiny hair.

EAST MEETS WEST

Junko Koshino is a Japanese designer of clothing and table accessories who is influenced by traditional Japanese values and the harmony of extremes, such as east and west, light and dark, day and night. Junko's teas reflect her values. One tea, unique in its simplicity, and the other more decorative, represent cultural influences other than those of Japan.

While a Japanese tea setting might look very simple, it takes imagination and skill to balance color, shape, and texture artfully. Wishing to create a cool, sleek mood, Junko chooses her green-and-black lacquer trays to frame the tea and sweets. The coolness is carried further through grasses, lotus leaves, and the green color of Matcha. One transparent sweet represents a mountain stream; the other, in the form of a saffron flower, adds a punctuation of color.

On another occasion, Junko uses decorative pieces collected from the Philippines and Indonesia along with her own tableware to create a multicultural tea. Unlike her Japanese tea, where beauty is attained by subtraction, she creates visual excitement by filling the table with crafts in tones of brown and with rustic textures, collected on her travels. She serves cakes made by her chef from Madagascar and her own blended black tea, which she has named Equal.

A BUSINESSMAN'S TEA

Washigaya has been a *tayu* establishment in Kyoto for over three hundred years. It is a place where a business executive can retreat for a couple of hours after a day in corporate life to eat and drink in the company of a tayu, a woman highly skilled in the arts of conversation, music, and dance. In a private room, dressed comfortably in kimono, he is offered a multi-course dinner ordered in from a restaurant, which includes several appetizers, two or three main dishes, a

japan

sweet, and tea. He is served and entertained by a tayu in opulent dress and astounding theatrical makeup. The two hours will cost one hundred thousand yen or about a thousand dollars.

PICNIC TEA

Teahouses were built with great care to suggest the simplicity of a small, humble hut found in the forest. They were constructed in quiet, idyllic settings to encourage enjoyment of nature and to bring calmness—small structures ideal for the tea ceremony or even casual entertaining. Keijakuan, the teahouse at Hakusasonso in Kyoto, one of the national treasures of Japan, was built by the artist Kansetsu Hashimoto in the garden world he created over a period of thirty years, starting in the early part of this century. His family still lives at Hakusasonso.

Tae Hashimoto, the artist's granddaughter-in-law, entertains with fanciful picnics, preparing them in the main house and carrying them to the teahouse in ceramic, lacquer, and bamboo containers. For a summer picnic she has prepared fresh fava beans with *daitokuji-fu* (fried tofu) and *satoimo* (sticky potato), assorted tempura, noodles and fish sauce, pickles, and rice balls wrapped in *nori* (seaweed). *Mizuyokan*, a Kyoto sweet wrapped in bamboo leaves, is served from a watermelon. In true Japanese style, Tae gives equal thought to color, texture, form, and flavor, as well as taste. She favors roasted green tea for her outdoor party, which is prepared and served from a lacquer tea basket.

The teahouse, situated at the south side of the pond, is surrounded by stone walks, pines, flowering trees, and moss-covered rocks. Fresh water splashes out of a bamboo spout next to the teahouse. It is a cool setting for informal picnics packed in baskets wrapped in cotton fabric, a charming way of presenting a surprise picnic and delighting guests as they discover the contents. Natural elements suit the rustic setting; bamboo serves as teapot and cups.

Tae's meals are movable feasts. At the other side of the pond, the atelier, a spacious room with views of the garden all around, provides a change to indoor entertaining. As is customary in Japan, the food is always fresh and seasonal. Green tea is often an ingredient in Japanese dishes, as in *ochazuke*, which is a combination of rice and a desired topping such as pickles or roasted salmon, over which hot green Houjicha tea is poured. Tae serves it as a light snack at any time, but some women give the tea-saturated dish to their husbands late at night to calm their stomachs after an evening of excessive drinking.

A COUNTRY TEA

Tea with *tsukemono* (pickles) is an old country habit going back to the days when a woman's cooking skills were judged by her pickles. She would serve them with tea at any time of day. Pickles are traditionally the ending to a meal, following the rice, adding a "home-cooked" touch, and are included in picnics, hikers' snacks, and lunches on the road. Tadashi and Kazuko Morita are antique dealers who follow the old customs. Their lunch table is prepared with an antique linen ikat kimono fabric, vintage Imari porcelain teacups, wooden saucers, and a plaid-patterned ceramic teapot. Pickled horseradish, eggplant, and cabbage are served in a bamboo basket along with seaweed-wrapped rice, balanced with a translucent bean paste sweet enclosed in a bamboo leaf. The roasted flavor of Houjicha offsets the tartness of the pickles.

THE TEA BREAK

The taste of Japan is in a bowl of *ocha* (green tea). With its fresh, slightly astringent qualities, green tea is the most refreshing of all the teas. It is produced from the leaves of the same tea bush as black teas; the difference is in the processing. The green tea leaves are steamed immediately after picking to destroy enzymes in the plant, preventing oxidation and leaving the leaf green with all its natural vitamins.

Green tea is particularly refreshing after sports and outdoor work. Farmers rest during the day with tea, often with an accompanying sweet such as *kusadango*, made of bean, grass, and rice powders. Gardeners set aside their clippers for a cup of Houjicha and rice cakes. It has added nutrition taken with *yuba*, which is made of bean curd skin formed in a square and tied up with a strip of seaweed. It is cooling and balances with sweet green tea kebabs, and it is warming by the fire in a country house, where a family slips off its shoes and kneels face to face around the irori for its green tea break.

Simple handmade crafts of wood, bamboo, straw, paper, stone, clay, and textiles typify Japanese culture as much as green tea. One of the most remarkable folk arts of Japan is textiles. Antique kimono weaves in the much loved blue-and-white linen and vintage obi (kimono sash) prints are resurrected and used on the table, giving them a new life.

Artists and writers take an intellectual tea break with a thirty-minute tea in a formal style, not unlike that of the tea ceremony. Four or five people are invited to tea for the purpose of discussing art and literature. The tea is prepared meticulously, the utensils placed just so, and the equipment selected to please the guests. A delicate summer flower is in pleasing contrast to its rustic bamboo container. The shell-shaped cookies are another homage to the season.

BENTO BOX TEA LUNCH

In Japan, long-distance train travelers are sustained by small meals prepared and neatly positioned in wood or lacquered boxes. They can be purchased at train stations and carried along on the journey. The boxes are kept as a souvenir of the trip. They are prepared for schoolchildren as well, their version of the lunch box, and are convenient for picnics. With tiny compartments constructed inside, *bento* boxes keep each part of the meal separate and tidy.

At The Tea Box at Takashimaya in New York City, bentos are popular at lunchtime. Every day, chef Ellen Greaves creates intriguing combinations for these traditional serving boxes. This one includes house-smoked salmon with napa cabbage flavored with preserved bean curd, shrimp and scallops with *wasabi* potato salad, chicken slices with curled pickled vegetables seasoned with black and white sesame seeds, and Jasmine tea rice. A cup of Sencha is the tea choice.

SHRIMP, SCALLOPS, AND POTATO SALAD WITH WASABI MAYONNAISE BENTO

Makes 4 servings

WASABI MAYONNAISE

1 large egg yolk, at room temperature

1 tablespoon fresh lime juice

1 tablespoon wasabi paste

$1/2$ teaspoon rice vinegar, preferably brown rice vinegar

1 cup peanut oil

Salt to taste

2 pounds small potatoes, preferably Fingerling or Yukon Gold, well scrubbed

8 ounces medium shrimp

1 tablespoon unsalted butter

1 tablespoon peanut or vegetable oil

8 ounces sea scallops, patted dry with paper towels

Salt and freshly ground black pepper to taste

Prepare the mayonnaise: Place the egg yolk, lime juice, wasabi, and rice vinegar in a medium bowl. Whisking constantly, slowly add the oil, dribbling it at first, then a little faster as the mayonnaise thickens. Let stand in the refrigerator for 30 minutes for the flavors to blend. Season with salt.

In a saucepan of boiling salted water, cook the potatoes until tender when pierced with a knife, about 20 minutes. Drain, rinse under cold water until cool enough to handle, and drain again. Slice the potatoes into $1/2$-inch-thick rounds and place in a medium bowl. Cool completely. Add the mayonnaise and toss gently to combine. Cover the potato salad and refrigerate until chilled, about 1 hour. (The salad can be prepared up to 8 hours ahead.)

In a saucepan of boiling salted water, cook the shrimp until just pink and firm, 2 to 3 minutes. Drain and rinse under cold water. Peel and devein the shrimp. Set aside on a plate.

In a large skillet, heat the butter and oil over medium-high heat until the butter foam subsides. Add the scallops. Cook, turning once, just until golden brown, about 3 minutes. Do not overcook. Using a slotted spatula, transfer to the plate with the shrimp. Season with salt and pepper. Cover and refrigerate until chilled, about 1 hour.

Spoon the potato salad into individual bento boxes or serving bowls and top with the shrimp and scallops.

Japan TEAS

"Tea is nought but this;
first you heat the water,
then you make the tea.
Then you drink it properly.
That is all you need to know."

SEN RIKYU (1522–1591)

Japan produces green teas exclusively in large gardens in the regions of Shizuoka, Mie, Kagoshima, Kyoto, Nara, and Saitama. They are taken without milk, sugar, or lemon—with the exception of iced Matcha, which is served with sugar syrup.

Gyokuro Japan's finest tea. The bushes are shaded with straw matting for three weeks before plucking in order to produce more chlorophyll and less tannin. Only the best leaves are used and great care goes into its production. It is pale celadon in the cup, with a subtle vegetal flavor with a sweet aftertaste and should be savored in the mouth before swallowing. It is as precious as a dewdrop, which is the translation of Gyokuro.

Matcha A powdered tea, used in the tea ceremony, which is prepared by whisking the powder to a froth in a bowl with a bamboo whisk. There are two types, strong Koicha and weaker Usucha. The latter contains as much vitamin C as two pounds of oranges. Matcha, considered a nourishing tea, is the color of jade in the bowl and has a mildly bitter taste. It makes an excellent iced tea.

Sencha A delicate blend of sweet and sharp grassy flavors.

Genmaicha Sencha mixed with roasted rice, which gives it a hint of popcorn flavor.

Houjicha A roasted tea with a nutty flavor. It contains little caffeine.

Kukicha A very light, low-caffeine tea made of roasted leaves and tea twigs.

brewing tea the japanese way

Matcha *For one serving:* Using a bamboo tea whisk, in a tea bowl, whisk together approximately one half-teaspoon powdered tea and six tablespoons boiling water. Whisk thirty times, until frothy.

Iced Matcha *For one serving:* Follow the basic Matcha recipe. Let cool, add ice, and serve with sugar syrup on the side. (Or, using the same proportions, blend the tea in a blender instead of whisking.)

Sencha *For three servings:* Rinse teapot with boiling water. Put two and a half teaspoons in the pot, add one and a half cups 170-degree water, and steep for a minute and a half.

Genmaicha *For three servings:* Rinse teapot with boiling water. Put one tablespoon tea in the pot, add one and a quarter cups 200-degree water, and steep for thirty seconds.

Houjicha, Kukicha *For three servings:* Rinse teapot with boiling water. Put one tablespoon tea in the pot, add one and a half cups 200-degree water, and steep for thirty seconds.

Gyokuro *For six tiny cups:* Rinse a small teapot with hot water. Put two teaspoons leaves in the teapot. Fill with hot water and rotate the pot counter-clockwise seven to ten times. Let steep for two minutes, rotate again the same number of times, and pour into cups.

Iced Gyokuro *For one serving:* Put one teaspoon leaves in a glass of cold water. The tea is ready to drink when the leaves have dropped to the bottom of the glass. (This tea keeps for one to two hours; after that, it will become bitter.)

india

"NOW LOOK AT THESE TWO INFUSIONS.
One is slightly cloudy and the other dead clear with
a green shade around the edge. The second is what
you want to aim at. You must keep on tasting such
infusions every few hours every day for a month
until you get the tastes firmly fixed on your palate."

A. R. RAMSDEN, *ASSAM PLANTER*, 1945

INDIA'S HISTORY OF TEA drinking dates back to primeval times, but was confined mostly to the populace around the vale of the Kamarupa, as Assam was called.

Commercial tea growing was first considered seriously under British rule. There was a great demand for the brew in Britain, and with the uncertainties of doing business with the Chinese, it was in Britain's interest to try planting in her colony. A major obstacle to such a venture was the powerful East India Company, which did all it could to stop tea cultivation in India, as it held a monopoly on the China tea trade and did not want any competition. But businessmen, Richard Twining among them, mounted extreme pressure on the government, and the lawmakers finally took action in 1833 and ended the East India Company's domination of the China tea trade. The ruling cleared the way for entrepreneurs to seek their fortunes in tea planting.

Major Robert Bruce, a Scottish soldier of fortune who had a flair for botany, was the first European to see an Assamese tea bush. He was introduced to it in 1823 by Maniram Dewan, a native nobleman who foresaw that his country's future lay in tea and wanted to play a role in it. Robert Bruce died in 1824 before he could benefit from his knowledge, but prior to his death he passed on all the information and the seeds he had gathered to his brother Charles.

Charles Bruce was convinced of the genuineness of the native Assam tea plant as early as 1825, having grown the samples his brother had sent him in his own garden, and he called it to the attention of the government in 1832, but his voice was lost to a more influential faction that insisted on the China *jat* (strain of tea). In 1834, the Tea Committee dispatched its secretary, George James Gordon, to China to study cultivation and manufacturing practices and to secure seeds, plants, and Chinese workmen. Many planters referred to the *Ch'a Ching* for further information on tea cultivation. In the end the native Assam plant won out, as the China jat was best suited to its own soil and climate.

On May 8, 1838, a small consignment of three hundred and fifty pounds of the first Assam tea was packed in eight wooden cases and shipped to London aboard the *Calcutta*. Nine months later, on January 10, 1839, the consignment was sold at India House in London with the East India Company as vendor. Euphoric tea experts praised the quality of the brew in the most glowing terms and it sold almost immediately at a very high premium. The Indian tea trade was established.

As a footnote, Maniram Dewan was hanged by the British on February 26, 1858 on false charges of conspiracy, when in truth it was because he had dared to start his own tea gardens. His fate was a warning to any other natives who might entertain the same idea.

Historians romanticized the early planters as derring-do demigods, the archetype of stiff-upper-lipped British officers who could "beard the lion in his den," stalwarts who battled dense jungles, tigers, leopards, mosquitoes, and malaria to establish the first gardens in Assam. No doubt the sorts who undertook the job were hardy, but they were also men with a lack of moral scruples and, for the most part, heavy-drinking fortune hunters who drove the thousands of native workers mercilessly.

The popularity of tea obsessed Europeans in the early 1860s. The promise of instant wealth in tea dizzied the minds of men who, without even the simplest knowledge of the rules of agriculture, headed into the tea business. Land-hungry entrepreneurs bought up and started gardens on impossible terrain. The price of seeds increased eightfold. Cheating and fraud were rampant. Unscrupulous operators would clear a few yards of jungle, plant some tea trees, and sell them as large gardens. Tea mania peaked in 1865, when the inevitable crash came, and the collapse that followed was just as dramatic and fast as the ascent. As the tea market plunged, expenses far exceeding earnings, owners abandoned their properties, unable to keep up. Gardens that had been bought for outrageous sums were sold for a pittance. The ruined planters pulled up stakes and left, abandoning their workers with no other means of support.

As in all instances in the rise and fall of business cycles, there is a winner for every loser, and within ten years new owners started up the gardens again and even ventured to other parts of India they thought might be suitable for tea growing. There were hardships in overseeing the clearing of dense jungles, building roads in extreme heat and torrential rain, planting, fertilizing, plucking, pruning, and transplanting for new gardens. In the factory, fresh leaves were brought in twice a day from the garden to the withering room, where the leaves were spread on burlap and left to dry for eight to ten hours, depending on the humidity. The leaves were then passed to the rolling room, where they were crushed and twisted, releasing enzymes and essential oils, and from there to fermenting beds, where the color was carefully checked and an infusion was made for tasting. Next the leaves were fired with blasts of dry heat, giving off a potpourri of heady aromas. Finally, the leaves were taken to the sorting room, where they were cut, graded, and sorted by grades— Broken Orange Pekoe, Orange Pekoe, Orange Fannings, Flowery Orange Pekoe, etc. The finest were hand-graded with bamboo sieves. Each grade was put into its own bin and fired again, then packed for export. Throughout the process, attention to detail was the key to success.

As demanding as the work was, there were rewards and pleasures to be had too. Planters were provided with comfortable accommodations, fully staffed with all expenses paid, and they earned a generous salary with an added 5 percent commission on profits; in good years, the commissions far exceeded their salaries. The club was never far off. There was time for polo, tennis, golf, fishing, and shooting, and at the end of the day, the "sundowner." As A. R. Ramsden describes his life in *Assam Planter*, "There was certainly much to do and no lack of variety, but you were fully paid by watching the whole place growing by leaps and bounds in front of your eyes. Buzzing from place to place in my car, poking about in the jungle with Mathaloo carrying my rifle, gathering mushrooms, finding orchids, and weighing up the possibilities of the many animal tracks down the nullahs— it was a great life!"

Tea was planted in the Dooars, Ceylon, Dehra Dun, Darjeeling, and the Nilgiri Hills in South India. The Indian jat was hardy, able to withstand the rigors of travel, and it flourished wherever it was grown. It seized markets that had been the domain of China for hundreds of years. Calcutta became the business capital of India's tea trade. The city built the largest tea warehouse in the country, as well as an auction house where tea was traded. Both are still in operation today. Indian tea made inroads into countries in all corners of the earth and made converts of coffee, cocoa, and *maté* (a favorite South American beverage) drinkers.

When India gained independence in 1947 and the British left, some aspects of the *raj* (British rule) remained. English was kept as the official language to assure harmony in a nation with fifteen major languages of its own, as was the parliamentary system of government—and the tea habit. Tea remains the preferred beverage throughout the twenty-three states and eight territories that make up the nation.

Tea in India

"I declare, a man who wishes to make his way in life could do no better than go through the world with a boiling tea kettle in his hand."

SYDNEY SMITH, ON OBSERVING A SERVANT CLEARING A PATH THROUGH A
CROWDED ROOM WITH A HISSING TEAKETTLE

stopping for tea

Black tea with milk and sugar is the national beverage of India. Tea is brewed on the street corners in cities and villages, in railroad stations, and in parks, offices, and bazaars: strong black tea from Assam, a slightly milder variety from the Dooars, milder-still Travancores from the Nilgiris in the south, and the prized, delicate teas from the dizzying slopes of Darjeeling. It is drunk from saucers in Gujarat and bowls in Rajasthan, brewed in a samovar and served in small metal cups in Kashmir, and poured into fine china in Maharashtra and glasses or tiny clay pots in Bengal.

In Calcutta, the center of the Indian tea trade, young boys squatting in tea stands watch over kettles of tea, buffalo milk, and sugar. Large teabags fashioned out of muslin are filled with a blend of dust tea and infused in vats of boiling water. Dust is the smallest leaf grade and infuses quickly. Once it is brewed, the boys keep the tea at the proper strength and temperature by adding more hot water, then more milk or sugar as needed, constantly adjusting the proportions. These *chai wallahs* (tea makers) are adept at keeping the brew at just the right point. From the kettles they pour the sweet tea into little clay pots, which are thrown on the ground after use, a practice both sanitary and ecological. Other tea wallahs peddle tea in kettles around the open markets and railroad stations. Over the cacophony of street noises, "Chai! Chai!" is heard. For half a rupee, tea can be purchased from chai wallahs in the Maidan (a park) in Calcutta. The infused tea is poured into a brass pot along with milk and sugar and kept hot all day over a charcoal burner. For another two rupees, *jhal moori*, a tasty tea snack, can be bought from the moori wallah, who carries his ingredients in a flat basket and sets up shop in the park. Jhal moori consists of puffed rice, tomato, cucumber, chickpeas, and boiled sliced potato spiced with coriander, green chiles, coconut chips,

masala (spices), salt, mustard oil, and tamarind water, all mixed together in a metal pot and wrapped in newspaper.

All over India, tea shops stacked with wooden boxes of tea cater to tea drinkers, many of whom fancy their own blends. As the customer approaches, the shopkeeper is often already in the process of mixing several teas into the favored blend. No instructions are necessary; he knows his clientele. At Aap Ki Pasand, a serious tea establishment in New Delhi, tea connoisseurs are invited to taste teas in a little sanctuary at the back of the shop. With the growth of the middle class in India, better teas are increasingly in demand, putting the burden on the tea planters to produce more to satisfy both domestic and export needs—but there is only so much land suitable for growing tea.

At truck stops throughout India, tea is ordered according to distance to be traveled. Truckers order one-hundred-mile or four-hundred-mile teas: The longer the trip, the stronger the tea. The milk-and-sugar tea is made in large pots and served in glasses that have been cleaned by pouring boiling water into them and throwing it out across the stone tea counter. Sometimes *gur*, raw brown sugarcane, is used to sweeten tea. Some who live in smog-polluted cities eat gur to cleanse their throats, breaking off bits to eat from a flat cake and following it with water. The gur acts as a sort of blotting paper. Tea with milk and gur is a nourishing drink and for the poor, that and a piece of bread is an affordable meal.

The attractive tearooms found in the grand hotels are busy during the afternoon tea hours. In Bombay, savories and sweets accompany pots of tea at The Taj, and vintage Irani cafés like Sassanian still serve tea and *mawa* cakes, but in India tea begins at home.

TAJ BOMBAY MASALA SANDWICH

Makes 1 sandwich

2 slices firm white bread

2 teaspoons unsalted butter, at
  room temperature

1½ tablespoons mango
  chutney

2 ounces sharp Cheddar cheese,
  thinly sliced

1 small boiling potato, cooked and
  thinly sliced

2 thin slices ripe tomato

1 thin slice onion

¼ teaspoon chat masala
  (available at Indian grocers)

Freshly ground black pepper
  to taste

Position a broiler rack 6 inches from the source of heat and preheat the broiler.
Toast the bread on 1 side. (Leave the broiler on.)

Spread the untoasted side of 1 slice of bread with the butter. Spread the
untoasted side of the other slice with the chutney. Cover both slices of bread with
the cheese. Return to the broiler and broil until the cheese is melted and bub-
bling, about 2 minutes.

Top 1 slice of bread with the potato, tomato, and onion. Sprinkle with the chat
masala and pepper. Cover with the second slice, cheese side down, and press
lightly. Cut in half with a sharp knife and serve immediately.

india

taking tea

THE BED TEA

Each day in India starts with a cup of "bed tea," the first of many to be consumed throughout the day. In a Gujarat village, a sculptor rises at 4:30 in the morning and takes his first milky tea of the day outside on a swing. All is quiet as he sips the warm brew under a dark, star-studded sky. Carved wooden swings are common in Gujarat. They hang from ceilings indoors and out, playful and relaxing settings for tea. In this part of India, tea spilling over into the saucer signifies the relaxed nature and generosity of the Gujarati, never holding back, always giving more.

In Jodhpur, Maharaj Swaroop Singh takes his bed tea in his dressing room or on the veranda of his Ajit Bhawan Palace Hotel. He drinks a special tea made with fenugreek, tulsi leaves, and ginger that is recommended for diabetes and arthritis. Waiters at Ajit Bhawan bring the bed tea to guests. During the morning hours, with their heads wrapped in yards of color-drenched cotton, they scurry along the paths of the Palace Hotel carrying teapots and cups on little tables.

Out in the Rajasthan desert, camel drivers start the day with a bowl of tea. It is their custom to share one bowl of tea, passing it around until it's finished. The tea is brewed with plenty of milk and sugar. It is accompanied with *chapati* (flatbread) and fresh spring onions.

FENUGREEK TEA

1 tablespoon fenugreek seeds

10 fresh tulsi leaves (available at Indian grocers) or basil leaves

1-inch piece ginger, peeled

2 cups water

Wedge of lime

Combine the fenugreek, tulsi, ginger, and water in a saucepan and boil until the liquid is reduced to 1 cup, about 10 to 15 minutes. Serve with lime.

RAJASTHAN TEAS

In the colorful desert state of Rajasthan, savories such as *samosas*, deep-fried pastries with spicy meat or vegetable fillings, and *golguppas*, filled with *jeera pani*, are popular snacks. Festively wrapped in silk tie-dyed fabric, the golguppas are easily prepared by buying the little puris, poking a hole in them with the thumb, and filling them with any desired chutney. Samosas are eaten all over India, varying in taste from region to region. Dotted around the state are fairy-tale palaces dating from ancient India, when silver teas were served in marbled rooms filled with princely furniture. Tea was brewed in silver pots that were stamped with paisley designs or molded into whimsical animals, then poured into silver teacups and accompanied by silvered sweets such as *kaju katli*, ground cashew nuts and sugar made into a paste, rolled out, cut into desired shapes, and frosted with a thin layer of edible silver.

SAMOSAS

Makes about 30 samosas

PASTRY

2 cups all-purpose flour

$^1/_2$ teaspoon salt

$^1/_2$ cup vegetable shortening, chilled

Approximately $^2/_3$ cup cold water

FILLING

4 medium boiling potatoes, (1 pound) well scrubbed

2 tablespoons vegetable oil, preferably sunflower oil

1 medium onion, chopped

1 teaspoon minced ginger

1 small hot chile pepper (such as serrano), seeded and minced

2 garlic cloves, minced

$^1/_2$ cup thawed frozen peas

$^1/_2$ teaspoon ground coriander

$^1/_2$ teaspoon garam masala

$^1/_2$ teaspoon ground cumin

2 tablespoons chopped fresh cilantro

$^1/_2$ teaspoon salt

CILANTRO-MINT CHUTNEY

2 cups packed fresh cilantro leaves with stems

$^1/_2$ cup packed fresh mint leaves

$^1/_2$ cup water

$^1/_4$ cup fresh lime juice

2 scallions, trimmed

2 tablespoons minced ginger

1 small hot chile pepper (such as serrano), seeded

1 teaspoon sugar

$^1/_4$ teaspoon salt

Vegetable oil for deep-frying

Prepare the pastry: In a medium bowl, combine the flour and salt. Using a pastry blender or two forks, cut in the shortening until the mixture resembles coarse meal. Gradually add water until the dough is moist enough to hold together when pinched between two fingers. Shape the dough into a disk, cover with plastic wrap, and let stand at room temperature for 15 minutes.

Prepare the filling: In a saucepan of boiling salted water, cook the potatoes until tender when pierced with the tip of a knife, about 25 minutes. Cool, peel, and cut into $1/4$-inch cubes.

In a large skillet, heat the oil over medium heat. Add the onion and cook until golden, about 5 minutes. Add the ginger, chile pepper, and garlic and stir for 1 minute. Add the potatoes, peas, coriander, garam masala, and cumin and stir until well combined. Stir in the cilantro and salt. Cool completely.

Prepare the chutney: In a food processor fitted with the metal blade, combine all of the ingredients and process until smooth. Transfer to a small bowl, cover, and refrigerate until ready to use.

To assemble the samosas, pinch off about 2 tablespoons dough and roll into a ball about $1^1/_2$ inches in diameter. (Keep the remaining dough covered.) On a lightly floured work surface, flatten the ball and roll out to a 6-inch-wide circle. With a sharp knife, cut it in half to make 2 semi-circles.

Moisten the straight edge of 1 semicircle with cold water. Lift up the ends of the straight edge to meet and overlap slightly. Press the seam closed to seal, forming a cone. Place about 1 teaspoon of the cooled filling into the cone. Pinch the top of the cone shut, pressing with the tines of a fork to seal. Place the filled samosa on a baking sheet. Repeat with remaining dough and filling. (The samosas can be prepared up to 4 hours ahead, covered with plastic wrap, and refrigerated.)

Preheat the oven to 200°F. Pour enough oil into a large deep skillet to reach 1 inch up the side and heat to 360°F. In batches, without crowding, fry the samosas, turning once, until golden brown, about 6 minutes. Transfer the samosas to a paper towel–lined baking sheet and keep warm in the oven while frying the remaining samosas. Serve hot with chutney for dipping.

KASHMIRI TEA

In the lush, green, northern state of Kashmir, the garden of India, rich in lakes with views of snow-covered peaks, the first tea of the day is prepared in a samovar. First charcoal is dropped into its chimney and around it, then the samovar is filled with water. Once the coals get going and the water comes to the boil, a loose green tea called Bombay Tea is added with a little sugar, crushed cardamom, and almonds. For special guests, a pinch of saffron from local crocus flowers is sprinkled in too. Once prepared, the spiced tea, called *kahva*, is drunk throughout the day, but the first morning one is always served in *pyals*, handleless metal cups, which are wrapped in small napkins. The tea is sipped slowly, warming one's hands as one drinks.

A huge variety of flatbreads to accompany tea are baked in clay ovens. Kashmiris eat bread and tea for breakfast and again at the four o'clock meal. Pieces of *bakirkhani*, a dark bread, and *kulcha*, a light one, both topped with poppy seeds, are broken off and dunked in the tea. Some breads are flavored with sesame seeds, others, like *schout*, are slightly salty. There are doughnut-like soft breads and sweet buns, *girda*, *krep*, and *shermal*—the range is endless.

CLUB TEA

When the British ruled India, they brought to the country their language, justice system, clubs, love of sports, and, of course, the tea habit. In Calcutta, Bombay, Delhi, and up at the hill stations, exclusive sporting clubs were established by the British, duplicating institutions started in the mid-nineteenth century in England. Homes away from home, these clubs provided comfort and recreation to the men in service in the colonies, as well as congenial settings for their families. Many of them still exist. Club life centers around sports, the bar, and the dining room, as clubs in the old days were homes to bachelors and provided a place for them to entertain. Standard Anglo-Indian fare was and is on the menu of every club. Afternoon tea served in wood-paneled rooms, on shady verandas, or out on manicured lawns is accompanied by club sandwiches, toasts grilled with toppings of garlic, green chiles, and grated cheese, and, always, spicy pakoras, samosas, and English cakes. Tea planters established clubs too, like The Darjeeling Club and High Range Club in Munnar, with its exclusive men-only bar where tea planters who have held a thirty-year membership have the honor of hanging their hats. The oldest ones belonged to A. W. John and W. A. Lee, members from 1894–1936 and 1895–1925 respectively. The club tea is Tata's high-grown top station tea, grown and produced on the high ranges above Munnar. Tata,

High Range Club

j Garden Retreat, Coonoor

an environmentally conscious Indian conglomerate. owns the land on which their tea is produced and keeps the area undeveloped and green. leaving room for the native elephants and ibex to roam freely. Originally planted by the British. Tata has maintained the early tea planters' traditions. The wives of planters are active in the club social life and take the responsibility of looking after the workers' housing. sanitation. and day-care. To some extent. their husbands' promotions depend on their good work.

The tea pluckers are women. while the heavier work such as pruning and planting is left to the men. The women are paid thirty-five rupees a day plus housing. medical benefits, and a ration of rice and cereals. Other benefits include education. day-care. club recreation. and their own vegetable gardens. The men earn forty-one rupees a day.

TAJ GARDEN RETREAT CLUB SANDWICH

¹/₂ **clove crushed garlic**

¹/₄ **cup grated cheddar or any hard cheese**

2 slices bread

1 jalapeño pepper

Mix garlic and cheese together and spread on bread. Make sandwich and grill under broiler. Garnish with sliced green jalapeño pepper.

TEA PLANTER'S TEA

The life of the early British planters was one of adventure and hard work, requiring a healthy constitution and adaptability. The weather could be harsh and diseases such as the deadly blackwater fever were common. Knowledge of agriculture, engineering, and management skills were requirements. The long hours began at dawn, with no definite ending time. But there was time for sports and the amusements of club life, and for managers, there was a cozy bungalow to live in, such as Ladbroke House, a turn-of-the-century planter's bungalow in Munnar. Teas are prepared in the old kitchen, where the house chef makes cheese sandwiches and bakes chocolate cake, strawberry tarts filled with the club ladies' jam, and coconut biscuits from handed-down recipes. Water is heated on the old wood-burning stove and as soon as Tata's orthodox tea—GBOP, Good Broken Orange Pekoe—is ready, it is served on the "sit out."

LADBROKE HOUSE COCONUT BISCUITS

Makes about 42 cookies

8 tablespoons (1 stick) unsalted
  butter, at room temperature

$1/2$ cup sugar

$1^1/2$ cups all-purpose flour

$2/3$ cup dried coconut (available at
  natural food stores)

3 tablespoons canned unsweetened
  coconut milk or whole milk

$1/4$ teaspoon salt

Position the racks in the center and top third of the oven and preheat the oven to 350°F.

In a medium bowl, using a hand-held electric mixer set at medium speed, cream the butter and sugar until light in color and texture, about 2 minutes. Stir in the flour, coconut, coconut milk, and salt.

On a lightly floured work surface, roll out half of the dough about $1/4$ inch thick. Using a 2-inch round cookie cutter (or any desired shape), cut out cookies and place about $1/2$ inch apart on the baking sheets. Gather up the scraps of dough and knead them into the remaining dough. Repeat the rolling and cutting until all of the dough is used.

Bake, switching the positions of the baking sheets halfway through baking, until the cookies are lightly browned around the edges, about 12 minutes. Transfer to wire cake racks to cool completely. (The cookies will keep, stored in an airtight container, for up to 5 days.)

A PARSI TEA

The Parsis came to India from Persia in the eighth century to escape religious persecution. They settled in Bombay and became traders, shipbuilders, bankers, and industrialists. The Parsis had an affinity for Western culture and collected fine silver from England, porcelain from France, and glass from Italy, mixing it with collectibles from the East. At Naheed Sorabjee's Sunday tea, there is a subtle blend of East and West, sweet and sour. French pastries, Parsi doughnuts called *bhakra*, and warm date *ghari* satisfy the sweet tooth. The rolled savory, *patrel*, adds the piquant note. A full-bodied Kangra tea, grown in the hills in the northwestern part of India, south of Kashmir and west of Tibet, complements both.

A TIFFIN TEA

Casual, tasty tiffin teas consist of sweet and savory finger food served picnic-style. Sujaya Menon covers her table with banana leaves and spreads it with spicy mixed nuts, crisp deep-fried plantains and potatoes, honey-filled *jelabi*, and *uppama* with coconut chutney. Uppama is a savory South Indian cereal made of semolina spiced with onions, chiles, ginger, mustard seeds, and curry leaves. Tea is served in stainless steel cups and bowls. The tea is poured from cup to bowl to cool it, then back into the cup to drink.

IDLIS AND TEA

Idlis are one of the treats of South India. Traditionally they are served at breakfast or as a mid-morning snack, along with a spicy sauce and chutneys. From humble house to Chettinad Palace, they are a favorite of the south. To make idlis, the chef at the Malabar Hotel in Cochin makes a batter of ground parboiled rice and split peas and leaves it to ferment overnight, then steams it in round molds and serves the fluffy, pancakelike cakes with *sambar* (split peas and potato sauce) and tomato and coconut chutneys. The South Indians like their tea as strong as coffee. A robust Assam blend satisfies them.

SOUTH INDIAN IDLIS

2 cups white, long grain rice (uncooked)

1 cup urad dal

salt to taste

Soak rice and dal separately in cold water for five hours. Grind rice to rough paste. Grind dal to fine smooth paste. Mix both together, add the salt and keep covered for at least three hours. Boil water in an idli steamer (or use a steaming basket set inside a colander lined with cheesecloth, making sure idlis are above water in steaming pan). When done, cut idlis into desired shapes. Pour the idli batter into steamer containers lightly oiled to prevent sticking. Cover with lid and steam 15–20 minutes. Serve hot with chutney and sambar.

Coconut Chutney

$^1/_2$ coconut, grated

1 jalapeño chile

Small piece ginger

1 teaspoon mustard seeds

$^1/_2$ teaspoon urad dal, crushed

A few curry leaves

Grind above ingredients to a rough paste. Sauté in vegetable oil the mustard seeds, urad dal, and curry leaves. When mustard seeds pop, blend mixture into coconut paste.

A TROPICAL TEA

Down in Cochin, rich in spices and tropical fruits, typical tea accompaniments are made of coconut and bananas, which are abundant around this southern seaport on the Arabian Sea. Coffee is popular in the south, but Cochin, the tea trading center of South India, has a tea tradition. Tea is auctioned here on Tuesdays and Thursdays with all the important tea brokers present.

Sarala Menon takes tea on her veranda, which looks out onto one of the inland waterways of Cochin. She serves steamed tea sweets on banana leaves including *pootu*, a cylindrical sweet made of a mixture of rice flour and grated coconut steamed in hollow bamboo, a rice flour dumpling called *kozhakatta*, and *nendhra pazham* (steamed bananas). After tea she and her guests take *pan*, which is a mixture of betel nut and spices wrapped in betel leaf. It is pleasant to chew and is a digestive.

Coconut sweets are numerous in the south of India, their fresh whiteness cooling in the tropical climate. Coconut *burfi*, made with milk, butter, and sugar, and *kinnathappam*, a moist sweet consisting of rice, coconut, sugar, and salt are typical white tea desserts.

BURFI

Makes 12 candies

½ cup milk

2 cups sugar

2 tablespoons unsalted butter

1½ cups sweetened flaked coconut

Raisins for garnish (optional)

In a heavy-bottomed 3-quart saucepan, bring the milk, sugar, and butter to a boil over medium heat, stirring constantly to dissolve the sugar. Attach a candy thermometer to the side of the saucepan, reduce the heat to medium-low, and continue cooking, without stirring, until the mixture reaches 238°F, the soft ball stage. Remove from the heat. Stir in the coconut and let stand for 5 minutes. Using a wooden spoon, beat until the mixture is thick and cream-colored, about 3 minutes.

Butter an 8- by 4-inch loaf pan and line the bottom with waxed paper. Spread the coconut candy evenly in the pan and cool completely. Invert the candy onto a work surface, remove the waxed paper, and cut into rectangles. If desired, garnish each candy with raisins.

Churutt (left); *kozhakatta, puttu* (center);
nendhra pazham, steamed bananas (above);
South Indian *idlis* (below)

India TEAS

"Thank God for tea! What would the world do without tea? How did it exist? I am glad I was not born before tea."

SYDNEY SMITH (1771–1845)

India mainly cultivates black tea, although some green is produced. The tea gardens are in Darjeeling, Assam, the Dooars, Terai, Kangra, Mandi, Dehra Dun, The High Range in Munnar, and the Nilgiri hills. Indian black teas can be taken with milk and sugar.

Assam Teas Strong and well-rounded teas with rich aroma and flavor. They are used in blended teas and are excellent for the morning.

Darjeeling Teas Quality depends on the weather conditions during its growth and the garden from which a particular Darjeeling comes. Margaret's Hope, Mim, Castleton, Thurbo, and Rungneet tea gardens are among the well known. Teas from the first flush are rare and cause much excitement when they come on the market, and command a good price at auction. The young first-flush teas (March through April) are light and slightly green. The second flush (May through June) is the largest harvest and produces teas with a distinctive muscatel flavor. The third flush (September through October) yields desirable mellow teas.

Dooars Teas Slightly less pungent than Assam teas. They are flowery, ideal for the morning.

Nilgiris, the Travancores Bright, fruity teas. The best are similar to their counterparts in Sri Lanka.

GINGER TEA FOR COUGHS AND COLDS

1-inch piece ginger, peeled and
   crushed

1 cup water

$1/8$ teaspoon black tea leaves

Simmer the ginger in the water for 2 to 5 minutes. Pour over the tea leaves and brew to desired strength.

TULSI TEA FOR COUGHS

8 fresh tulsi leaves

4 peppercorns

1 teaspoon peeled and
   crushed ginger

1 teaspoon honey

$1^1/_2$ cups water

Combine all of the ingredients in a saucepan and simmer until reduced to 1 cup.

TURMERIC-GINGER TEA FOR COUGHS

Pinch of turmeric

1-inch piece ginger, peeled and
   crushed

1 cup milk

Combine all the ingredients in a saucepan and simmer for 3 minutes.

MASALA TEA TO AID DIGESTION AND FOR COUGHS

10 cardamom pods

2 cinnamon sticks

12 whole cloves

$1^1/_2$-inch piece ginger, peeled and
   crushed

6 cups water

$2^1/_2$ teaspoons black tea leaves

Combine the cardamom, cinnamon sticks, cloves, ginger, and water in a large saucepan and bring to a boil. Cover and simmer for 5 minutes. Add the tea leaves, turn off the heat, and cover until everything settles, about 2 minutes. Strain into a teapot and serve with warm milk and sugar.

brewing tea the classic way

Stainless steel tea balls or mesh baskets that fit in the teapot are practical as they allow the tea leaves to be removed as soon as the tea is brewed, thereby keeping the second and third cups of tea at the same strength as the first. The tea ball should not be more than half-filled, to allow the leaves to expand. Use a tea cozy to keep the teapot hot.

Bring cold water (three quarters of a cup per cup of tea) to a boil. Heat the teapot by rinsing it out with boiling water. Put one teaspoon tea leaves per cup in the heated teapot. Brew for three to five minutes for black and oolong teas, two minutes for green tea. (Use two teaspoons tea leaves per cup.)

Tastes vary, and more or less tea in the teapot and steeping time is a matter of personal choice. Too little tea and brewing time results in a flat, insipid tea, too much of both becomes a stewy, bitter tea.

ICED GINGER-LEMON TEA

3 tablespoons peeled and grated
  ginger

Grated zest of 2 lemons

2$\frac{1}{2}$ cups cold water

$\frac{1}{2}$ cup sugar

$\frac{3}{8}$ cup lemon juice

1 tablespoon black tea (Darjeeling,
  Assam, or Ceylon)

Mint sprigs

In a saucepan, combine the ginger, lemon zest, and cold water. Bring to a boil and simmer for 15 minutes. Strain into another saucepan. Add the sugar and bring to a boil, stirring to dissolve the sugar. Strain into a bowl. Add the lemon juice, cool, and refrigerate.

To make the iced tea, make a pot of black tea, using 3$\frac{1}{2}$ cups of water and letting it brew for about 2 minutes. Strain, cool, and add to the ginger concentrate with a few sprigs of fresh mint.

To serve, pour into glasses and dilute with water as necessary, depending on desired strength. Garnish with mint sprigs.

To decaffeinate tea: Infuse the tea leaves for three minutes in boiling water. Pour off the water and infuse again according to the basic method.

To brew tea for a crowd: Make a concentrate of two thirds of a cup tea leaves and one quart boiling water. Steep five minutes. stir. and strain into a large teapot. To serve. add one cup boiling water to two table-spoons of this concentrate. Makes 24 cups.

sri
lanka

"AND LET US BLESS THOSE SUNNY lands so far away across the sea whose hills and vales gave fertile birth to that fair scrub of priceless worth, which yields each son of Mother Earth a fragrant cup of tea."

ANONYMOUS, 1899

CEYLON, KNOWN AS SERENDIP by Arab traders in medieval times (hence the word *serendipity*), is a tropical paradise between the Arabian Sea and the Bay of Bengal, just thirty miles from the Indian mainland. Although the country is now known as Sri Lanka, its tea is still called Ceylon, the name synonymous with fine teas. There is ample vegetation on the lush island, plenty of rice fields, splendorous beaches, and ruins of ancient Buddhist cities hidden in its dense jungles. On a train ride from Colombo to the hilly tea country in the interior, coconut, cacao, rubber, and cardamom trees dominate the landscape, their scents pervasive, along with frangipani, sandlewood, jackfruit, and mango. As the train approaches Kandy, the cultural and spiritual capital, which is at sixteen hundred feet in the central highlands, magnificent views of the tea estates materialize with dramatic suddenness through the rain and mist. The luxuriant green tea gardens undulate over the crowns and slopes of the foothills.

The island was a major producer of coffee until a killer blight, *Hemileia vastatrix*, struck in 1869 and soon after destroyed the bountiful coffee crop—an industry that at its peak had represented scores of millions of dollars to the nation's coffers. Dead coffee trees were stripped and shipped to England, where they were cut up and turned into tea-table legs. Ruined planters, burghers, and laborers fled in despair to seek their fortunes elsewhere, many to Malaysia. A small band of diehards refused to give up, and, in a desperate gamble against what appeared to be insurmountable odds, they planted tea seeds from Assam in the wastelands where coffee had once flourished. The tea that resulted was excellent; its aroma, fragance, and color compared favorably with the best of its kind in the world. A new industry appeared to be on its way, but there was a problem with labor: The local Buddhist people refused to do menial, back-breaking work for the planters. As a result, immigrants were brought in from South India. The laborers were paid very little and their accommodations were inadequate, but they worked hard and without them there would not have been the successful crop of about a thousand acres that was harvested in 1875. That figure skyrocketed to three hundred thousand acres by 1900.

At the time of the coffee catastrophe, Thomas Lipton, an enterprising grocer from Glasgow (he eventually owned a grocery empire extending to London), was in the market for a new venture and dispatched an agent to look over the possibilities in Ceylon. As a result, Sir Tea, as he was later called, a man with a keen instinct for opportunity, was one of the early beneficiaries of the island's new-found success. He bought plantations for half the price he had expected to pay and was in the tea business by 1891.

The tea-growing region is around the center of the southern end of the island, east of Colombo, an area of fertile plains rising gradually to misty mountains which reach altitudes of seven thousand feet. From this lush area come Ceylon teas carrying the names of the estates where they are grown, from the districts of Nuwara Eliya, Uva, Dimbula, Pettiagalla. Orange Pekoe, Lipton's mainstay, is not a garden name, but indicates a leaf grade. English Breakfast teas, such as Twinings, are blends of Ceylon teas.

The turnaround of Sri Lanka's fortunes with the death of one industry and the birth of another in its ashes is remarkable. Today, tea is the primary business of Sri Lanka and the industry is the country's largest employer. The island exports more tea than any other nation on earth.

Tea in Sri Lanka

"Freshly plucked tea-leaf has the same spicy smell as growing leaf, resembling that of ginger root or the concentrated
smell of hay with the acrid part predominating."

J. M. SCOTT, *THE GREAT TEA VENTURE*, 1965

the tea estates

Just off the coast of South India in central Sri Lanka, the Assam and China
jat rooted and produced black Ceylon tea, a major world source of fine teas.
Since 1875, tea has been harvested on this tropical island in the wet southwestern foothills, where leaves are plucked weekly, and on the northeastern
hills reaching heights of six thousand feet, where the choicest tea is grown.
Each day sari-wrapped women, heads covered in white fabric that falls
across their shoulders to protect them from the burning sun, stand waist-high
in tea bushes, nimbly plucking the leaves and filling their baskets. At pre-
cisely four-thirty in the afternoon, one by one, they pour the day's pickings
onto the scales, have their tally cards marked, and collect their chits.

The planters and tea estate managers are busy all day with field, factory,
and office duties. With the exception of modern machinery that has stream-
lined the business, processing tea leaves has remained much the same since
its beginning—withering, rolling, fermenting, drying, sifting out stalks, and
sorting by grades. Grading identifies the leaf size and is mainly for the benefit of the tea blender and packer. Ceylon's OP, Orange Pekoe, is the largest
leaf grade and most expensive tea although the leaves yield less juice; FP,
Flowery Pekoe, is a smaller leaf grade and has the best aroma; BOP, Broken
Orange Pekoe, even smaller, has the best flavor and more juice; and BOPF,
Broken Orange Pekoe Fannings, is a smaller leaf grade than BOP but has the
same qualities. At the end of the line is Dust, which is used in teabags.

Toward six or seven in the evening, the tea manager returns to his bungalow. As in India, bungalows come with the job and are built in similar style,
as the early planters in Ceylon were also English, Scottish, or Irish. One early
tea planter wrote, "I loved that bungalow more than any of the other habita-
tions I have infested before or since. It fitted me exactly, and above all it spelt
freedom with a capital F. With a good dog and no lack of books from home,

the talk of loneliness out in the jungle being bad for a man and sending him slightly crackers is absolute nonsense . . . I had more than enough to keep my mind occupied."

Planters' clubs sprang up along with tea estates. The Hill Club in Nuwara Eliya, at the foot of the island's highest mountain and with a name synonymous with Sri Lanka's champagne teas, was founded in 1876 by three British planters. The teas are on a par with Darjeelings, light-colored, delicate, and flavorful, just right for the afternoon.

taking tea

BREAKFAST TEA

It's quiet, the air is fresh. Little by little, sounds invade the hush, a distant clatter of crockery, footsteps, snatches of voices. In the early morning, south of Colombo, a weekend by the sea is just beginning and there's time to linger with a pot of strong-flavored English Breakfast tea, thick, crunchy toast, and fruit jam.

English Breakfast tea is a blend of Ceylon teas or Ceylon mixed with Indian. It is the first tea of the day in Sri Lanka and in many other parts of the world.

LUNCH TEA

At the oldest hotel in Asia, The Galle Face in Colombo, dating from 1864, teatime is any time on the cool loggia. Ceiling fans above and ocean breezes beyond keep the air moving in the tropical heat.

At lunch, tea with hoppers is an institution. Hoppers, a variation of pancakes or crepes, were a favorite of the British tea planters. They are made of rice flour, coconut milk, sugar, salt, and yeast and are accompanied by curry and a spicy sauce. A Broken Orange Pekoe from the Uva estates has the intense flavor and aroma to enhance the spicy lunch. Hoppers smeared with jam are a popular sweet tea snack.

The Hill Club

The Villa

COCONUT HOPPERS

Makes about 10 hoppers

Approximately 3 cups canned unsweetened coconut milk

1 teaspoon sugar

1 teaspoon active dry yeast

2 cups all-purpose flour

³/₄ teaspoon salt

Nonstick vegetable cooking spray

In a measuring cup, combine $1^2/_3$ cups of the coconut milk with the sugar. Sprinkle in the yeast and let stand for 3 minutes. Stir well to dissolve the yeast.

Stir the flour and salt together in a medium bowl. Stir in the yeast mixture to make a thick batter and beat well. Cover with plastic wrap. Let stand in a warm place until the batter is doubled in volume, about $1^1/_2$ hours.

Gradually stir in 1 cup of the remaining coconut milk to make a thin batter. Cover again and let stand until the surface of the batter is covered with tiny bubbles, about 30 minutes. Stir in the remaining $^1/_3$ cup coconut milk to make a pourable batter.

Preheat the oven to 200°F. Heat a 10-inch wok or nonstick skillet over medium heat (see Note). Spray the wok with vegetable oil spray. Pour a scant $^1/_2$ cup of the batter into the wok, immediately rotating it to allow the batter to spread, thinly coating the bottom of the pan. Cover and cook the hopper until the sides are crispy and golden brown and the center is set, about 2 minutes. Using a rubber spatula, transfer the hopper to a baking sheet. Keep warm in the oven while cooking the remaining hoppers.

NOTE: Sri Lankan cooks make hoppers in an unusual wok-shaped utensil that gives them a distinctive shape and texture. Making the hoppers in a skillet gives them a crepe-like appearance. They are equally delicious prepared either way.

(right)
The Galle Face Hotel

AFTERNOON TEA

Tissawewa Rest House nestles in the ancient capital of Anuradhapura, where settlement began in 500 B.C. The quiet guest house is a stone's throw from ancient Buddhist ruins, where the oldest tree in the world still bears leaves.

A graceful waiter in a white *lunghi* silently arrives on the verandah at Tissawewa with tea, curds, and bun cakes. Curds, or yoghurt, are made of buffalo milk, which ferments in terra-cotta pots. It is rich and dense. Sweet jaggery syrup, made of brown sugar, is swirled over the top. After spoonfuls of the clotted sweet, deep-fried bun cakes are washed down with a fruity Pettiagalla Orange Pekoe.

tea in the east

Ceylon TEAS

"A tea with a touch of flavor is described as having a good nose. A hay flavor is one which often precedes the autumnal. A weedy flavor is reminiscent of dried grass, and is undesirable."

C. R. HARLER, *THE CULTURE AND MARKETING OF TEA,* 1933

The teas of Sri Lanka, called Ceylon teas, are black teas. The best and the lightest are grown in altitudes of four to six thousand feet. The lower-grown teas are less delicate and have a stronger flavor. As with Darjeelings, they are sold under the name of the garden in which they are grown. The teas are taken with milk and sugar.

Although other districts produce quality teas in season, teas from the following districts are highly recommended.

Nuwara Eliya, OP An exquisite, slightly lemony afternoon tea.

Uva Highlands, FOP A full-bodied, fragrant breakfast tea.

Dimbula, BOP A flavorful, fruity morning tea.

(right)
The Villa

the language
of tea

"Goodness is a decision for the mouth to make."

LU YU, *CH'A CHING*, 780

Agony of the leaves: The unfurling of the leaf in boiling water.

Biscuity: An agreeable robust quality associated with Assam teas.

Bite: The astringent characteristic of black teas that makes them refreshing.

Body: The strength of a tea and its weight on the tongue.

Bright: Sparkling red liquor, a quality of fine teas.

Brisk: Tea that is lively, not flat.

Dull: Liquor that is neither clear nor bright.

Flat: Liquor that is neither brisk nor pungent.

Full: Strong tea with no bitterness.

Gone off: Tea that is tainted or stale.

Liquor: The infusion.

Peak: The point in tasting a black tea when its body, flavor, and astringency are felt. (Greens and oolongs immediately reveal their characteristics.)

Pointy: A liquor that reveals a desirable characteristic, such as appealing aroma or brightness.

Pungent: Astringent.

Rough: Harsh liquor.

Self-drinking: A tea that needs no blending or flavoring and fulfills all requirements of a good brew on its own.

Stewy: A bitter liquor from overbrewing; or one with no peak because of poor firing.

Sweet: A light liquor.

Tarry: A smoky aroma and flavor.

Thin: Liquor with neither color nor body.

Weedy: The vegetative aroma and flavor of green teas. Negatively, thin, "cabbagey" black teas.

Winey: The mellow quality of Darjeelings or Keemuns, developed by aging six months or more.

bibliography

Dutta, Arup Kumar. *Cha Garam!* Guwahati, Assam, India: Paloma Publications, 1992.

Goodwin, Jason. *A Time for Tea.* New York: Alfred A. Knopf, 1991.

Harler, C. R. *The Culture and Marketing of Tea.* London: Oxford University Press, 1933.

Okakura, Kakuzo. *The Book of Tea.* Tokyo, New York, and London: Kodansha International, 1989.

Pratt, James Norwood. *The Tea Lover's Treasury.* Berkeley, Calif.: 101 Productions, 1982.

Ramsden, A. R. *Assam Planter.* London: John Gifford Limited, 1945.

Scott, J. M. *The Great Tea Venture.* New York: E. P. Dutton & Company, Inc., 1965.

Sen XV, Soshitsu. *Tea Life, Tea Mind.* New York and Tokyo: Weatherhill, 1979.

Ukers, William H. *All About Tea.* New York: The Tea and Coffee Trade Journal Company, 1935.

Yu, Lu. *The Classic of Tea.* Translated by F. R. Carpenter. Boston: Little, Brown and Company, 1974.

source guide

CHINA

TEAHOUSES, TEA SHOPS
China National Tea Museum
Shuangfeng Village, Long Jing Road
Hangzhou, Zhejiang Province
Tel. 724221

Humble Administrator's Teahouse
Souzhou, Jiangsu Province

Hu Pao Teahouse
outside Hangzhou

Lakeview Teahouse
West Lake, Hangzhou

Ping Feng Teahouse
outside Hangzhou

hong kong, kowloon

The Best Tea House Company
Cheung Sha Wan Plaza
833 Cheung Sha Wan Road, Kowloon
Tel. 743-9915

Fook Ming Tong Tea Shop
Prince's Building, Ice House Street,
Central
Tel. 521-0337

Flagstaff House Museum of Tea Ware
10 Cotton Tree Drive, Central
Tel. 869-0960
Daily 10-5 (closed Wednesday)

Hong Kong Teaism Center
98 Argyle Street, Kowloon
Tel. 761-4998

Jabbok Tea Shop
98 Argyle Street, Kowloon
Tel. 713-7936

Luk Yu Tea House
24-26 Stanley Street, Central
Tel. 523-5464

Mr. Chan Tea Room
1 Wellington Street, Central
Tel. 868-9288

Ngan Ki Heung Tea Co., Ltd.
(Tea Zen)
290 Queen's Road, Central
Tel. 544-1375

Tai Koon-Lock Cha Tea Shop
290 Queen's Road, Central
(Ladder Street entrance)
Tel. 805-1360

Wing Kee Tea Merchants
26 Cochrane Street, Central
Tel. 544-3594

AFTERNOON TEAS
Grand Hyatt
1 Harbour Road
Tel. 588-1234

Hilton
2 Queen's Road
Tel. 523-3111

Mandarin Oriental
5 Connaught Road, Central
Tel. 522-0111

The Peninsula
Salisbury Road, Kowloon
Tel. 366-6251

JAPAN

TEAHOUSES, TEA, WAGASHI AND MOCHI SHOPS

tokyo

TEAHOUSES

Mantei (teahouse in garden)
1-19-19 Kitizyozi Minami-mati
Musasino-shi
Tel. 2246-9871

Shogesu Do
4-22-12 Nishi-Azabu Minato-ku
Tel. 3407-0040

Suzuki (tea ceremony rooms and
tea garden)
1-15-4 Zingu-mae Shibuya-ku
Tel. 3404-8007

Tea Leaves
Matsuya Department Store
3-6-1 Ginza Chuo-ku
Tel. 3567-1211 (closed Thursdays)

Takemura
1-19 Kanda Suda-cho, Chiyoda-ku
Tel. 3251-2328

Nezu Institute of Fine Arts (teahouse in
garden)
6-5-1 Minami-Aoyama, Minato-ku
Tel. 3400-2536

WAGASHI (SWEETS) AND MOCHI (BISCUITS)

Kikuya
5-13-2 Minami-Aoyama, Minato-ku
Tel. 3400-3856

Toraya (also teahouse)
4-9-22 Akasaka, Minato-ku
Tel. 3408-4128

Matsuzaki Senbei
4-3-11 Ginza Chuo-ku
Tel. 3561-9811

kyoto

TEAHOUSE

Shin Shin Do
Imadegawa Higashi-oji Sakyo-ku
Tel. (O75)701-4121

TEA SHOP

Ippodo Tea Co., Ltd.
Teramachi-dori Nijo-noboru, Nakagyo-ku
Tel. (075)211-3421

WAGASHI (SWEETS)

Gensui
Abura-kozi Nijyo kudaru
Nakagyo-ku
Tel. (075)211-0739

Toraya (also teahouse)
Karasuma Nishi Hairu
Ichijo dori, Kamigyo-ku
Tel. (075)441-3111

CHANOYU (TEA CEREMONY)

Kano Shojuan
Philosopher's Walk
Tel. (075)751-1077
10 A.M.–4:30 P.M. (closed Wednesdays,
in Japanese only)

Urasenke Foundation (Tea Ceremony)
Ogawa dori, Kamigyo-ku
Tel. (075)451-8516
Thursdays 1 P.M. or 3:30 P.M. (call before
noon to reserve)

uji

Kanbayashi Tea Museum
Uji-Myoraku Uji-shi
Tel. (077) 422-2513 10 A.M.–6 P.M.
(closed Friday)

INDIA

TEA ROOMS, TEA, TEA ACCESSORIES, AND SWEETSHOPS

bombay

AFTERNOON TEA

The Taj Mahal Hotel—Sea Lounge and poolside
Apollo Bunder
Tel. 2023366

Gaylord
Veer Nariman Road

Sassanian & Co. (Irani Café)
1st Marine Street. Dhobi Talao

TEA ACCESSORIES

Popli & Popli
Stevens Street. Apollo Bunder

Central Cottage Industries Emporium
34 Shivaji Maharaj Marg. Apollo Bunder

calcutta

AFTERNOON TEA

Taj Bengal
34-B Belvedere Road. Alipore
Tel. 248-3939

Tollygunge Club Ltd.
Tel. 473-4741

TEA SHOP

Dolly's
Shop G-62
2 Gariahat Road (South)

TEA INFORMATION

Tea Board
14 Biplabi Trailokya Maharaj Sarani
Tel. 25-1411

BENGAL SWEETS

K. C. Das
Esplanade Road East

Gupta's
Park Street

Ganguram
Shakespeare Sarani

Girish Dey
56 Ramdulal Sircar Street

TEA ACCESSORIES

The Good Companions
13 C Russell Street

darjeeling

AFTERNOON TEA

The Windemeer Hotel
Observatory Hill
Tel. 2841/397

The Darjeeling Club Ltd.
Town Center
Tel. 54349

new delhi

AFTERNOON TEA

The Taj Mahal Hotel
1 Mansingh Road
Tel. 3016162

Hotel Imperial
Janpath
Tel. 3325332

Aap Ki Pasand (and tea shop)
15 Netjaji Subhash Marg
Tel. 326-0373

TEA ACCESSORIES, TABLE LINENS

Central Cottage Industries
Emporium Janpath

FabIndia
N-Block. Greater Kailash

The Shop
10 Regal Building,
Connaught Circus

Lepakshi Handcrafts Emporium
B-6 State Emporia Complex

Tandon of Lucknow
Palika Bazaar, Connaught Place

SWEETS
Malik
Connaught Place

Bengali Sweet House
Gole Market, Connaught Place

Gantiwalla
Chadni Chowk (Old Delhi)

Naim Chand Jain's
corner Dariba Kalan (Old Delhi)

TEA INFORMATION
Darjeeling Tea Bureau
11, Kaka Nagar Market
Tel. 462-2442

jodhpur

TEA AND TABLE LINENS
Ajit Bhawan Palace
Usha Enterprises—Shop
Tel. 37410

the nilgiri hills

Coonoor, Ootacamund (Ooty)

AFTERNOON TEA
Taj Garden Retreat
Church Road, Coonoor
Tel. 643-010

Taj Savoy Hotel
77 Sylks Road, Ootacamund
Tel. 4142

**TEA INFORMATION,
NILGIRIS**
Tea Board of India, Calcutta

the high range munnar

AFTERNOON TEA
The High Range Club
Contact Tata Tea Limited
Tel. 30561

TEA INFORMATION
Tata Tea Limited
P. O. Box 9
Tel. 30561

udaipur

AFTERNOON TEA
Lake Palace Hotel
Pichola Lake
P. O. Box No. 5
Tel. 23241

TEA ACCESSORIES
Motilal R. Minda
at Lake Palace Hotel

SRI LANKA

colombo

AFTERNOON TEA
Galle Face Hotel
Box 63
Tel. (941) 541010-6

The Hill Club
Nuwara Eliya
Tel. 052-2653

The Villa
Nos. 138/18 & 138/22, Galle Road
Bentota
Tel. (94) 72-30102

Tissawewa Rest House
Sacred City, Anuradhapura
Tel. 025-2299

TEA INFORMATION
Sri Lanka Tea Board
574, Galle Road, Colombo 3
Tel. 582236

The Ceylon Tea Promotion Bureau
P.O. Box No. 295, Colombo 3
Tel. 582121

UNITED STATES

new york

AFTERNOON TEA

Felissimo
10 West 56th Street
Tel. (212)247-5656

Kelley & Ping
127 Greene Street
Tel. (212)228-1212

T
Prince and Mercer Streets
Tel. (212)925-3700

The Tea Box
Takashimaya Department Store
693 Fifth Avenue
Tel. (212)350-0100

Toraya
17 East 71st Street
Tel. (212)861-1700

CHANOYU (TEA CEREMONY)

Urasenke Inc.
153 East 69th Street
Tel. (212)988-6161

TEA SHOPS

McNulty
109 Christopher Street
Tel (212)925-9905

Porto Rico Importing Company
201 Bleecker Street (main store)
(212)477-5421
Mail order outside New York City
1-800-453-5908

Ten Ren Tea and Ginseng Co., Inc.
75 Mott Street
Tel. (212)349-2286

Angelica Herb & Spice (Herb Teas)
147 First Avenue
Tel. (212)677-1549

california

Chado Tea Room
8422½ West Third Street
Los Angeles
Tel. (213)655-2056

Imperial Court
1411 Powell Street
San Francisco
Tel. (415)788-6080

connecticut

Chaiwalla
1 Main Street
Salisbury
Tel. (860)435-9758

north carolina

Silk Road Teahouse
456 West Franklin Street
Chapel Hill
Tel. (919)942-1533

washington

The Tea Cup
2207 Queen Ann Avenue
Seattle
Tel. (206)283-5931

TEA BY MAIL

Grace Tea Company, Ltd.
50 West 17th Street
New York, N.Y. 10011
Tel. (212)255-2935

John Harney & Sons
11 East Main Street
Salisbury, Connecticut 06068
Tel. 1-800-TEA-TIME

O. H. Clapp & Company, Inc.
47 Riverside Drive
Westport, Connecticut 06880
Tel. (860)226-3301

Sarum Tea Company
P. O. Box 796
Salisbury, Connecticut 06068
Tel. 1-800-342-1922

Silk Road Teas
P.O. Box 287
Lagunitas, California 94938
Tel. (415)488-9017

Tea Luxuries
(Tea and Tea Accessories)
1411 Powell Street
San Francisco, California 94133
Tel. 1-800-567-5898

The East Indies Company
Lebanon, Pennsylvania 17042
Tel. 1-800-220-2326

Upton Tea Imports
(Tea and Tea Accessories)
231 South Street
Hopkinton, Massachusetts 01748
Tel. 1-800-234-8327

Mark T. Wendell
P. O. Box 1312
West Concord, Massachusetts 01742
Tel. (508)369-3709

HERBALS

TransPacific Health Products
7217 Gulf Boulevard
St. Petersburg, Florida 33706
Tel. 1-800-336-9636

index

Page numbers in *italics* refer to recipes.

samosas, *102–103*
samovars, 46, 49, 94, 104
sandwich:
 green tea–marinated chicken, *16*
 Taj Bombay masala, *99*
Sassanian tearoom, 98
scallops, shrimp and potato salad with
  wasabi mayonnaise bento, *83*
scented tea, 40
Sencha tea, 64, 82, 84, 85
Sen Rikyu, 58, 70
"Servant Rules," 2
Shanghai, 34, 37
shrimp:
 scallops and potato salad with wasabi
  mayonnaise bento, *83*
 steamed dumplings with bamboo
  shoots and, *27*
Sichuan hills, 2, 38, 44
Silvery Tip Pekoe tea, 15, 39
Singh, Maharaj Swaroop, 100
smoked tea, 40, 47
Sorabjee, Naheed, 110
Souchong:
 Lapsang, 15, 40
 Tarry, 15
South Indian idlis, *112*
Souzhou, 15
Spain, 6
spice cake, Russian Tea Room, *50–51*
squid, stir-fried noodles with shiitake
  mushrooms, pork, and, *31*
Sri Lanka, xiii, 9, 47
 Buddhism in, 124, 134
 coffee blight in, 124, 125
 immigrant labor in, 124
 tea-drinking in, 129, 134
 tea workers in, 126
 see also Ceylon tea
steamed dumplings with shrimp and
  bamboo shoots, *27*
stir-fried noodles with shiitake
  mushrooms, squid, and
  pork, *31*
storing tea, 41
Story of the Flower House, The (Lu
  Shusheng), 24
Suez Canal, 9
Sumatra, xiii

Sung dynasty, 4, 19, 24, 34, 44, 55
 whipped tea in, 4–5, 37, 58

Tai Koon–Lock Cha Tea Shop, 28
Taiwan, xiii, 15, 46
Taj, The, 98
 Bombay masala sandwich, *99*
Takashimaya, 82
Tale of Hajji Mahommed, The
  (Ramusio), 47
Tao Hongjing, 24
Tarry Souchong tea, 15
Tata, 104, 106, 107
tea:
 aged, 15, 40
 Assam, 88, 94, 112, 116, 126
 black, xii, 6, 33–34, 49, 88, 90, 94,
  110, 112, 116, 124, 129, 134, 136
 Bolei (Pu Erh), 15, 25, 28, 33, 40
 Bombay, 104
 botanical classifications of, xii
 brewing of, 28, 40, 44–45, 49, 85, 94,
  118, 119
 brick, 5, 6, 44, 45, 54, 58
 ceremony, Japanese, 55, 58, 65, 70,
  78, 84
 Ceylon, 49, 124, 125, 129, 134, 136
 chamomile, 49
 Ching Wo, 19, 39
 compressed orange, 15
 Darjeeling, 94, 116, 129
 decaffeinated, 119
 Dooars, 90, 94, 116
 earliest records of, 2
 English Breakfast, 125, 129
 Fancy Formosa Oolong, 15, 39
 fenugreek, *100*
 fermentation (oxidation) of, xii, 6
 flavored, 5–6, 12, 15, 33, 40, 47
 Flowery Orange Pekoe, 89, 126
 Formosa Lapsang, 15
 Genmaicha, 64, 85
 ginger, for coughs and colds, *117*
 gong fu, 28
 green, xii, 6, 28, 38, 49, 64, 78, 84,
  85, 104
 Gunpowder (Pearl Tea), 24, 38
 Gyokuro, 58, 64, 84, 85

bibliography

Dutta, Arup Kumar. *Cha Garam!* Guwahati, Assam, India: Paloma
   Publications, 1992.

Goodwin, Jason. *A Time for Tea.* New York: Alfred A. Knopf, 1991.

Harler, C. R. *The Culture and Marketing of Tea.* London: Oxford
   University Press, 1933.

Okakura, Kakuzo. *The Book of Tea.* Tokyo, New York, and London:
   Kodansha International, 1989.

Pratt, James Norwood. *The Tea Lover's Treasury.* Berkeley, Calif.: 101
   Productions, 1982.

Ramsden, A. R. *Assam Planter.* London: John Gifford Limited, 1945.

Scott, J. M. *The Great Tea Venture.* New York: E. P. Dutton & Company,
   Inc., 1965.

Sen XV, Soshitsu. *Tea Life, Tea Mind.* New York and Tokyo: Weatherhill,
   1979.

Ukers, William H. *All About Tea.* New York: The Tea and Coffee Trade
   Journal Company, 1935.

Yu, Lu. *The Classic of Tea.* Translated by F. R. Carpenter. Boston: Little,
   Brown and Company, 1974.